Prayers

THAT PREVAIL

for your
Children

Prayers
THAT PREVAIL

for your
Children

A PARENT'S & GRANDPARENT'S
MANUAL OF PRAYERS

By
Clift Richards & Lloyd Hildebrand

Victory House Publishers
Tulsa, Oklahoma

PRAYERS THAT PREVAIL FOR YOUR CHILDREN
The Parent's & Gandparent's Manual of Prayers
Copyright © 1994 by K & C International, Inc.
ISBN 0-932081-39-8

Published by Victory House, Inc.
P.O. Box 700238
Tulsa, Oklahoma 74170
(918) 747-5009

Cover Design by: "Sigma Graphic Design"

Contents

Books By
Clift Richards & Lloyd Hildebrand

PRAYERS THAT PREVAIL
(The Believer's Manual of Prayers)

PRAYERS THAT PREVAIL FOR AMERICA
(Changing a Nation Through Prayer)

PRAYERS THAT PREVAIL FOR YOUR CHILDREN
(A Parent's & Grandparent's Manual of Prayers)

A LITTLE BIT OF GOD'S WISDOM AND WIT
(A Treasury of Quips and Quotes about Life and Love from God's Infinite Wisdom)

A LITTLE BIT OF GOD'S WISDOM & WIT FOR MEN
(Gems of Wisdom for Living a Happy and Successful Life)

GOD'S GUIDELINES FOR PARENTS & CHILDREN

A successful parent studies the art of speaking in the spirit of love, by striving to make his whole life an attractive example of what he has taught. (Andrew Murray)

Leadership by Example

Modeling behaviors and values that represent our faith is the very best way to teach our children the principles of God's Word. By this means, God's ways become normal to them. Edmund Burke wrote, "Example is the school of mankind, and they will learn at no other." Being a good example to our children is one of the most important choices we can make as parents, as Joshua pointed out in the Old Testament:

> *And if it seem evil unto you to serve the Lord, choose you this day whom ye will serve; whether the gods which your fathers served that were on the other side of the flood, or the gods of the Amorites, in whose land ye dwell:* **but as for me and my house, we will serve the Lord.** *(Josh. 24:15, emphasis ours)*

We need to pray for our children and for those children we know whose parents have not made the important choice to serve the Lord. God wants each one to be saved. Sometimes, as Paul pointed out in his letter to young Timothy, children can be good examples for their parents and others, and in spiritual matters, they may need to take the lead:

> *Let no man despise thy youth; but be thou an example of the believers, in word, in conversation, in charity, in spirit, in faith, in purity. (1 Tim. 4:12)*

In each of these areas, parents must be good examples to their children. As Samuel Johnson pointed out, "Example is always more efficacious than precept."

Example in Word

In the parent-child relationship, as in all relationships, effective communication is vital. Positive communication with our children involves the following principles:

- Encouragement, not criticism

- Praising our children, not putting them down

- Constructive criticism, not condemnation

- Edifying our children, not belittling them

- Respecting our children, not discounting them

- Honoring God's name, never taking it in vain

- Reading God's Word to our children

- Studying the Bible in front of them

- Reading Christian books to our children

- Helping them to memorize Bible verses

- Blessing our children

- Praying for and with our children

- Teaching our children

- Listening to our children

- Playing with our children

- Counseling with our children

- Avoiding gossip, slander, judgment of others

- Expressing good attitudes toward authority figures

- Praising God

- Being thankful

- Involving ourselves with our children's interests

- Expressing our love to them

- Modeling conflict resolution in a healthy manner

These attitudes and actions are "better caught than taught." If we want loving children, we must provide them with an atmosphere of love in which to grow and flourish. If we want them to respect us, we must respect them. In all likelihood, our children will become like us in each of these areas.

Example in Conversation

The New International Version of the Bible uses the word "life" in place of "conversation." Paul is referring to one's life-style when he points to the need of being a good example in the area of "conversation." As parents, our style of living must be above reproach. Paul wrote, "Abstain from all appearance of evil. And the very God of peace sanctify you wholly" (1 Thess. 5:22-23).

The Christian life-style that we must demonstrate to our children is based upon godliness, righteousness and holiness. Some of its characteristics are listed by Paul:

> *Let all bitterness, and wrath, and anger, and clamour, and evil speaking, be put away from you, with all malice: And be ye kind one to another, tenderhearted, forgiving one another, even as God for Christ's sake hath forgiven you. (Eph. 4:31-32)*

The Ten Commandments, the Golden Rule, the Sermon on the Mount and many other passages of the Bible paint vivid pictures of what the Christian life-style actually entails. One key to living according to God's ways is found in these words of Jesus: "Abide in me, and I in you. As the branch cannot bear fruit of itself, except it abide in the vine; no more can ye, except ye abide in me. I am the vine, ye are the branches: He that abideth in me, and I in him, the same bringeth forth much fruit: for without me ye can do nothing" (John 15:4-5).

Abiding in Christ, and His abiding presence within us, opens the door to the fulfillment of God's purposes in our families. Paul wrote, "I can do all things through Christ which strengtheneth me" (Phil 4:13). As the Holy Spirit fills us, we become fruitful in our relationship with our children. The fruit of the Spirit enable us to live the Christian life-style in front of our children and others:

> *But the fruit of the Spirit is love, joy, peace, longsuffering, kindness, goodness, faithfulness, gentleness, self-control: Against such there is no law. (Gal. 5:22-23, NKJV)*

Example in Charity

Charity is love, and love is the theme of effective parenting. Without it, as Paul points out, we "...become as sounding brass, or a tinkling cymbal" to our children. Christian family life is based on love:

> *Husbands, **love your wives**, even as Christ also **loved the church, and gave himself for it;** That he might sanctify and cleanse it with the washing of water by the word, That he might present it to himself a glorious church, not having spot, or wrinkle, or any such thing; but that it should be holy and without blemish. So ought men to **love their wives as their own bodies. He that loveth his wife loveth himself.** For no man ever yet hated his own flesh; but nourisheth and cherisheth it, even as the Lord the church: For we are members of his body, of his flesh, and of his bones. For this cause shall a man leave his father and mother, and shall be*

*joined unto his wife, and they two shall be one flesh. This is a great mystery: but I speak concerning Christ and the church. Nevertheless let every one of you in particular **so love his wife even as himself**; and the wife see that she reverence her husband. Children, obey your parents in the Lord: for this is right. Honour thy father and mother; (which is the first commandment with promise;) That it may be well with thee, and thou mayest live long on the earth. And, ye fathers, provoke not your children to wrath: but bring them up in the nurture and admonition of the Lord. (Eph. 5:25-6:4, emphasis ours)*

As the husband demonstrates love for his wife in every conceivable way, an environment of love and caring is established in the home, enabling the children to obey more readily and the wife to reverence her husband. As H. Page Williams expressed it in his book, *Do Yourself a Favor: Love Your Wife*, when a husband sets the mood in the family by initiating love, everyone responds in positive ways!

Paul wrote, "The only thing that counts is faith expressing itself through love" (Gal. 5:6, NIV).

Example in Spirit

Jesus said, "But seek ye first the kingdom of God, and his righteousness; and all these things shall be added unto you" (Matt. 6:33). This commandment places high priority on spiritual values, and a family with parents who put God first is blessed indeed:

> *Blessed is every one that feareth the Lord;*
> *that walketh in his ways. For thou shalt eat the*
> *labour of thine hands: happy shalt thou be, and*
> *it shall be well with thee.* ***Thy wife shall be as a***
> ***fruitful vine by the sides of thine house: thy***
> ***children like olive plants round about thy table.***
> *Behold, that thus shall the man be blessed that*
> *feareth the Lord. (Ps. 128:1-4, emphasis ours)*

Happiness. Prosperity. Blessings. Fruitfulness. These rewards come to parents who place a high value on spiritual things. Their children shall become like olive plants (the most important type of tree in biblical times, because its fruit was used for food, fuel, light, carpentry, ointments, medicines, etc.). Children in such homes are a source of happiness and blessing; they fill the home with light, love and joy.

Example in Faith

God wants us to take Him at His Word, to stand upon His promises, to believe that He is the Giver of every good and perfect gift. (Be sure to read the section of this book entitled, "God's Promises for Parents and Children.")

William Wordsworth wrote, "By reason, blest by faith: what we have loved, Others will love, and we will teach them how." It is faith that enables us to love, and by loving our children we teach them the importance of faith. Faith and love are inseparable twins, like goodness and mercy.

It is when adverse circumstances confront the family, that parents reveal the true value of faith. They show their kids the power, victory and truth that come by way of faith.

> *For therein is the righteousness of God*
> *revealed from faith to faith: as it is written, The*
> *just shall live by faith. (Rom. 1:17)*

The example of faith is one of the most important values we ever impart to our children, for it is faith that will see them through the difficult times. Faith appropriates the promises of God in practical ways. Faith will restore broken dreams. Faith will bind up the broken heart and the prayer of faith will even heal the sick. A parent's consistent walk of faith provides children with a firm foundation on which to build their lives.

Example in Purity

Purity of heart leads to purity of life. As Jesus revealed, "Blessed are the pure in heart: for they shall see God" (Matt. 5:8). We want our children to keep themselves pure, and we show them how to do this by our example of purity. It comes as a result of washing in the Word of God:

> *Now ye are clean through the word which*
> *I have spoken unto you. (John 15:3)*

By meditating upon the Scriptures, hiding them in our hearts, studying them daily, praying their promises, and teaching them to our children, we bring purity to our lives, to our children and to our homes. The Word is a window through which we perceive:

> *Whatsoever things are true, whatsoever*
> *things are honest, whatsoever things are just,*
> *whatsoever things are pure, whatsoever things*

are lovely, whatsoever things are of good report;
if there be any virtue, and if there be any praise,
think on these things. (Phil. 4:8)

It is what we hold in our hearts that comes forth in our behavior. If we hide God's Word in our hearts, and if we focus on the qualities listed above, our lives will reflect those attributes. Our children will, therefore, be influenced to adhere to the same values.

Teaching Our Children

Once we are certain that our lives as parents truly reflect the values and truths we wish to convey to our children, they will be ready to receive our verbal instructions in righteousness.

And all thy children shall be taught of the
Lord; and great shall be the peace of your
children. (Isa. 54:13)

Peace comes to our children when we teach them the ways of the Lord. Once they experience the peace of mind and peace of heart that come to them by way of the Word, they will begin to seek God's truth on their own.

And these words, which I command thee this
day, shall be in thine heart: And thou shalt teach
them diligently unto thy children, and shalt talk
of them when thou sittest in thine house, and
when thou walkest by the way, and when thou
liest down, and when thou risest up. And thou
shalt bind them for a sign upon thine hand, and
they shall be as frontlests between thine eyes,

And thou shalt write them upon the posts of thy house, and on thy gates. (Deut. 6:6-9).

The key word in this passage may well be "diligently." Diligence and consistency are important aspects of godly parenting. Every child needs to know what his/her limits are, and parents must enforce the rules of the home consistently. Each child needs to know what will happen if they violate the rules. There is security in knowing where the boundaries are.

The purpose of Christian teaching is to disciple our children to become followers of the Lord Jesus Christ. Such followers must be obedient. Parents need to remind their children of this requirement, and consistently share with them the truths of God's Word. The wonderful result will always be:

Train up a child in the way he should go: and when he is old, he will not depart from it. (Prov. 22:6)

Correction

Correct thy son, and he shall give thee rest; yea, he shall give delight unto thy soul. (Prov. 29:17)

Far too often, parents interpret "correction" to mean "punishment." A better synonym for correction is "discipline," which means to train, disciple, teach. Through consistent correction, a parent can teach his/her child many important truths.

Correction, we need to remember, must be administered lovingly, fairly and consistently. *Never* correct your child in anger, because anger begets anger, and no one wants an angry child. Paul wrote:

> *And, ye fathers, provoke not your children to wrath: but bring them up in the nurture and admonition of the Lord. (Eph. 6:4)*

The goal of our parenting is to bring up our children in the nurture and admonition of the Lord. All of our modeling, our prayers, our teaching and our correction should keep this goal in mind. If this is our parental vision, God will bring it to pass, as long as we are faithful to do our part.

The Value of Children

> *The smell of my son is as the smell of a field which the Lord hath blessed. (Isaac, Gen. 27:27)*

> *Israel loved Joseph more than all his children, because he was the son of his old age. (Gen. 37:3)*

> *If I be bereaved of my children, I am bereaved. (Jacob, Gen. 43:14)*

> *Children are an heritage of the Lord: and the fruit of the womb is his reward. (Ps. 127:3)*

> *As arrows are in the hand of a mighty man; so are children of the youth. Happy is the man that hath his quiver full of them. (Ps. 127:4-5)*

*He that begetteth a wise child shall have
joy of him. (Prov. 23:24)*

A little child shall lead them. (Isa. 11:6)

*Whoso shall receive one such little child in
my name receiveth me. (Jesus, Matt. 18:5)*

*Out of the mouth of babes and sucklings
thou hast perfected praise. (Jesus, Matt. 21:16)*

*Whosoever shall offend one of these little
ones that believe in me, it is better for him that
a millstone were hanged about his neck, and he
were cast into the sea. (Jesus, Mark 9:42)*

*Suffer the little children to come unto me,
and forbid them not: for of such is the kingdom
of God. (Jesus, Mark 10:14)*

*I have no greater joy than to hear that my
children walk in truth. (3 John 4)*

Truly, children are a divine blessing in our lives.
Jesus loves children. The are inheritance we receive from
God. He rewards us with children. They bring happiness
to us. They give us joy. Sometimes they lead us, especially in areas like trust, truthfulness, innocence, purity,
honesty, faith and love. When we receive children, we
receive Jesus. The cries of children are perfect praise to
God. Childlikeness is a prerequisite to entering the
Kingdom of God. What a blessing our children are!

The Promise of Children

> *Thy seed shall be as the dust of the earth.*
> *(God to Jacob, Gen. 28:14)*

> *Her children arise up, and call her blessed.*
> *(Prov. 31:28)*

> *House and riches are the inheritance of fathers: and a prudent wife is from the Lord.*
> *(Prov. 19:14)*

> *In thee and in thy seed shall all the families of the earth be blessed. (Gen. 28:14)*

> *I will make thy seed as the dust of the earth: so that if a man can number the dust of the earth, then shall thy seed also be remembered. (Gen. 13:16)*

> *He maketh the barren woman to keep house, and to be a joyful mother of children. (Ps. 113:9)*

> *"As for me, this is my covenant with them," says the Lord. "My Spirit, who is on you, and my words that I have put in your mouth will not depart from your mouth, or from the mouths of your children, or from the mouths of their descendants from this time on and forever," says the Lord. (Isa. 59:21, NIV)*

To the righteous, God promises fruitfulness, blessing, prosperity, far-reaching influence, succeeding generations and joy. The lineage of a righteous family reaches into all generations, providing a godly influence in the lives of those who are yet to come.

The Effects of Godly Discipline of Children

> *He who spares the rod hates his son, but he who loves him is careful to discipline him. (Prov. 13:24, NIV)*

> *Discipline your son, for in that there is hope; do not be a willing party to his death. (Prov. 19:18, NIV)*

> *Train a child in the way he should go, and when he is old he will not turn from it. (Prov 22:6, NIV)*

> *Folly is bound up in the heart of a child, but the rod of discipline will drive it far from him. (Prov 22:15, NIV)*

> *Do not withhold discipline from a child; if you punish him with the rod, he will not die. (Prov 23:13, NIV)*

> *Discipline your son, and he will give you peace; he will bring delight to your soul. (Prov 29:17, NIV)*

> *Fathers, do not embitter your children, or they will become discouraged. (Col 3:21, NIV)*

Godly correction and discipline help our children in the following ways: it changes their behavior, it insures their future success, it removes foolishness from their hearts, it delivers them from hell, and it actually encourages them. Many make the mistake of not correcting their children consistently. Such a course results in the child becoming foolish, selfish, hopeless, unfaithful, and angry. The parent of a disobedient child experiences disgrace, but the parent of an obedient child has delight.

Instruction in Righteousness

My son, hear the instruction of thy father, and forsake not the law of thy mother: For they shall be an ornament of grace unto thy head, and chains about thy neck. (Prov. 1:8-9)

Hear, ye children, the instruction of a father, and attend to know understanding. (Prov. 4:1)

A wise son heareth his father's instruction: but a scorner heareth not rebuke. (Prov. 13:1)

A fool despiseth his father's instruction: but he that regardeth reproof is prudent. (Prov. 15:5)

All scripture is given by inspiration of God, and is profitable for doctrine, for reproof, for correction, for instruction in righteousness: That the man of God may be perfect, throughly furnished unto all good works. (2 Tim. 3:16-17)

Clearly, it is our responsibility as Christian parents to give instruction in righteousness to our children. The result of such instruction, based on the Word of God, will be wisdom, beauty, spiritual understanding, and good works in the lives of our children.

The Love of Jesus

When Karl Barth, the great theologian who wrote *Church Dogmatica*, reached his eightieth birthday, a reporter asked him, "Dr. Barth, in all your years of studying the Scriptures and theology, what is the most important thing you have ever learned?"

The octogenarian paused a moment, scratched his head, then answered, "I believe it is this: Jesus loves me, this I know, for the Bible tells me so."

As we pray with, sing to, teach and correct our children, let us be certain to get this all-important message through to them: JESUS LOVES YOU!

GOD'S PROMISES FOR PARENTS AND CHILDREN

But now, O Lord, thou art our father; we are the clay, and thou our potter; and we all are the work of thy hand. (Isa. 64:8)

God — the Model Parent

Our heavenly Father knows the challenges and joys inherent in parenthood. Like you, He wants the best for His children at all times. He'd like to see them avoid mistakes, be perfectly successful, healthy and happy. "Like as a father pitieth his children, so the Lord pitieth them that fear him" (Ps. 103:13).

Unfortunately, however, sometimes His children have rebelled against Him. Others have turned their backs on Him and His counsel. Still others have engaged in sibling rivalry, and all have been disobedient. God knows the hurts experienced by a parent who sees his or her child making unwise choices.

Each of us has been given a free will so that we can choose to worship, love, serve and obey our Father. He wants us to love Him of our own volition, out of our sense of need. This is the chief end of mankind — to know God and to enjoy Him forever. If we had been created to love

God automatically, naturally, it would not have been our choice to do so. Our Father wants His children to *choose* to love Him.

To those who make such a wise choice, God extends rich and precious promises. Some of these promises are for parents who know they need His wisdom and guidance to enable them to be effective mothers and fathers. And because God understands what it is like to parent children who have free wills, He clearly understands your dilemmas and frustrations. He knows how difficult it is for you to be a parent in these changing times, and He wants to help you. In fact, He has written a personal letter to you (the Holy Bible), and it contains practical advice and guidance that will equip you to face the issues of parenting with confidence and faith.

Prayers That Prevail for Your Children is based on the Bible. Our Father in heaven is delighted when His children take Him at His Word. He loves to see His children basking in the light of His precepts and principles. He even invites us to take our stand upon His promises, trusting Him to bring about the necessary changes in our lives as parents and in the lives of our children. He commits himself to you: "But my God shall supply all your need according to his riches in glory by Christ Jesus" (Phil. 4:19).

How do you obtain those promises? Through faith and prayer. God expects parents to pray for their children. Such intercession brings eternal results. When we pray according to the will of God, we can be sure that God hears our prayers and He will always answer them. "This is the confidence that we have in him, that, if we ask any thing according to his will, he heareth us: And if we know that he hear us, whatsoever we ask, we know that we have the petitions that we desired of him" (1 John 5:14-15).

To pray effectively, then, we need to form our prayers in line with the Bible. More specifically, we need to be sure that our prayers are in tune with God's promises. The whole counsel of God — His eternal will — is revealed in the Scriptures. If we pray according to the Word of God — indeed, if we pray the Scriptures themselves — we can be certain that we are praying in accord with the Father's will for us and our children. This style of praying, therefore, assures that God will hear us and answer our prayers, and "...whatsoever we ask, we know that we have the petitions that we desired of him" (1 John 5:15).

Each of the topical prayers for your child(ren) is based on the promises of God as they are revealed in the Bible. (For further insights concerning this exciting, powerful way of prevailing prayer, see our earlier works: *Prayers That Prevail — the Believer's Manual of Prayers* and *Prayers That Prevail for America — Changing a Nation Through Prayer.* Both are published by Victory House, Inc.)

Jesus himself recommended this approach when He said, "If ye abide in me, *and my words abide in you*, ye shall ask what ye will, and it shall be done unto you (John 15:7, italics ours). Clearly, when you pray for your child(ren) according to the truths of God's Word, as you keep on abiding in Jesus and letting His words abide in you, you will see lasting results in the lives of your child(ren).

God's Promises — Your Answers

Through this type of praying, you will be able to prevail in behalf of your child(ren). At the same time, several amazing blessings will come to you as you learn to live and pray this way:

● *You will be able to discern the will of God.* ("For the word of God is quick, and powerful, and sharper than any twoedged sword, piercing even to the dividing asunder of soul and spirit, and of the joints and marrow, and is a discerner of the thoughts and intents of the heart" — Heb. 4:12.)

● *You will grow in wisdom and knowledge.* ("My son, attend unto wisdom, and bow thine ear to my understanding: That thou mayest regard discretion, and that thy lips may keep knowledge" — Prov. 5:1-2.)

● *Your faith will accelerate.* ("So then faith cometh by hearing, and hearing by the word of God" — Rom. 10:17.)

● *Your love for your child(ren) will be cultivated.* ("And we have known and believed the love that God hath to us. God is love; and he that dwelleth in love dwelleth in God, and God in him" — 1 John 4:16.)

● *You will become fruitful in all that you do.* ("And he shall be like a tree planted by the rivers of water, that bringeth forth his fruit in his

season; his leaf also shall not wither; and whatsoever he doeth shall prosper" — Ps. 1:3.)

    ● *You will produce the fruit of the Spirit in
your dealings with your child(ren).* ("But the fruit
of the Spirit is love, joy, peace, longsuffering,
gentleness, goodness, faith, Meekness, temperance: against such there is no law — Gal. 5:22.)

All these blessings, and many more besides, are
yours to enjoy as a child of God. They will be passed on
to your children as well — a far better inheritance than
silver and gold. As the Father uses the tools of His Word
and believing prayer to renew your thinking, reshape your
attitudes and help you in every way, your child(ren) will
reap enormous benefits, both from your example and from
answered prayer!

In the Light of Eternity

What things really count in the brilliant light of eternity? When someone is preoccupied with worries that
seem trivial to another, the latter person might be tempted
to say, " In the light of eternity it really doesn't matter." In
the final analysis, few concerns are significant when they
are brought into the penetrating light from beyond.

The issues and concerns related to parenting,
however, are matters that really do count in the light of
eternity. For many, parenting is the major responsibility of
their lives that has eternal significance. What we do with
and for our children will affect their destinies as well as the
lives and futures of succeeding generations. What could
be more important than parenting?

In view of this fact, prayer may well be a parent's most vital tool today. Through prayer, the mother or father is able to find that "safe place" in the Father's lap where one senses that God is bearing life's burdens, lifting all cares and surrounding the heart with love. *Prayers That Prevail for Your Children* will help you find that resting place Jesus invites you to discover:

> *Come unto me, all ye that labour and are heavy laden, and I will give you rest. Take my yoke upon you, and learn of me; for I am meek and lowly in heart: and ye shall find rest unto your souls. For my yoke is easy, and my burden is light. (Matt. 11:28-30)*

It is an exciting responsibility to be a parent. This role in life brings with it the promise of eternal rewards, and it offers great joy and happiness in this life as well. As Sir John Bowring wrote, "A happy family is but an earlier heaven."

God is there with you each step of the way. Practice His presence. Hold onto His hand. Speak to Him and let Him speak to you. Trust Him to bring good things into the lives of your child(ren). Paul's prescription for a happy, fulfilled life is applicable to parents and children today: "Rejoice evermore. Pray without ceasing. In every thing give thanks: for this is the will of God in Christ Jesus concerning you" (1 Thess. 5:16-18). Build your life and your prayers on His "exceeding great and precious promises" (2 Pet. 1:4).

Above All That We Can Ask

For all the promises of God in him are yea,
and in him Amen, unto the glory of God by us.
(2 Cor. 1:20)

What are God's specific promises for you and your family? First and foremost, He wants every member of your family to be saved. The Father's love for His children is incomprehensibly vast — so vast, in fact, that He sent His Son to become sin for us. (See 2 Cor. 5:21.) The best-known verse in the Bible declares this truth: "For God so loved the world, that he gave his only begotten Son, that whosoever believeth in him should not perish, but have everlasting life" (John 3:16). God has made His amazing love and grace available to us through His Son, Jesus Christ, and it is that love that enables us to become effective parents.

If you do not know Jesus Christ as your personal Lord and Savior, please take this opportunity to invite Him into you heart and life. By receiving Him through faith, you open the door to new life for each of your children.

But as many as received him, to them gave
he power to become the sons of God, even to
them that believe on his name. (John 1:12)

Pray now by confessing your sins to God. Ask Him to forgive you and to cleanse you from all unrighteousness. Let Him know that you believe in your heart that He raised Jesus from the dead, and you are now confessing that Jesus is your Lord and Savior, your only hope in this life and the next. Ask Him to wash you in the blood of

Jesus and tell Him that you are sorry for your sins. When you do this, you will become a totally new person.

> *Therefore if any man be in Christ, he is a new creature: old things are passed away; behold, all things are become new. (2 Cor. 5:17)*

Welcome into the family of God! You are now the beneficiary of God's great love. By trusting Christ by faith for salvation, you are now beginning an exciting adventure that will never end! The pathway begins with prayer, is paved by prayer and it ends with prayer. The promises of God are markers along the way.

Every Christian parent can claim this promise for his family:

> *And they said, Believe on the Lord Jesus Christ, and thou shalt be saved, and thy house. (Acts 16:31)*

God wants to see your child(ren) be born again. This book contains a prayer that expresses God's promises regarding the salvation of your child(ren). Pray it often, and trust God to bring it to pass. Your child(ren) will be saved!

Nurturing Discipline

> *Train up a child in the way he should go: and when he is old, he will not depart from it. (Prov. 22:6)*

Too often, the word "discipline" connotes punishment. Its true meaning center on training, not controlling or correcting.   God promises to see to it that your child(ren) will stay on track if you make sure you put them on the proper track through loving nurture, positive discipline and prayer.

Prayer is a parent's one recourse that cannot fail. It is a dynamic resource of energy. The words of William James ring true in the heart of every Christian parent: "Energy which but for prayer would be bound is by prayer set free and operates." Through prayer, we are able to find the energy we need to be consistent, caring parents at all times.

God's promise is clear:

He giveth power to the faint; and to them that have no might he increaseth strength. Even the youths shall faint and be weary, and the young men shall utterly fall: But they that wait upon the Lord shall renew their strength; they shall mount up with wings as eagles; they shall run, and not be weary; and they shall walk, and not faint. (Isa. 40:29-31)

The key to good discipline is consistency and stability. When modeled by a Christian parent as a result of his or her regular prayer life, such consistency becomes a place of security for a child or a young person. The child learns precisely what limits and expectations there are that demand his compliance.

Discipline that is backed by prayer, based on the promises of God's Word, leads to obedience in the life of a child. This is a primary parental goal; if a child learns obedience to his or her parent(s), he or she is better

prepared to obey God. Let us always keep in mind God's
promise to obedient children:

> *Children, obey your parents in the Lord:*
> *for this is right. Honour thy father and mother;*
> *(which is the first commandment with promise;)*
> *That it may be well with thee, and thou mayest*
> *live long on the earth. (Eph. 6:1-3)*

The Apostle Paul goes on to explain how parents can
help their children accomplish this goal:

> *And, ye fathers, provoke not your children*
> *to wrath: but bring them up in the nurture and*
> *admonition of the Lord. (Eph. 6:4)*

Anger always begets anger. Because this is true, no
discipline should ever be administered in anger. When our
focus is on punishment, our attitude may reflect anger, but
if our focus is always on what is best for our child(ren), our
attitude is shaped by love. Through prayer, a parent learns
how to take positive actions in behalf of his child(ren)
rather than always reacting with emotional outbursts. God
will help you to become pro-active rather than reactive as
you learn to pray His Word and claim His promises.

The Tender-Hearted Parent

In writing to the young church at Ephesus, the Great
Apostle shared godly principles and truths in an effort to
help Christians — members of the household of faith, the
family of God — learn how to get along together.

Those same principles and promises apply to family living in our world today:

> *Let all bitterness, and wrath, and anger,*
> *and clamour, and evil speaking, be put away*
> *from you, with all malice: And be ye kind one to*
> *another, tenderhearted, forgiving one another,*
> *even as God for Christ's sake hath forgiven you.*
> *(Eph. 4:31-32)*

Tender-heartedness is an attitude that is shaped by prayer and the Word of God. It is an attribute of empathy — the ability to feel and experience what another person feels and experiences. For parents, the ability to remember back to what it was like when we were children will help us to develop this kind of empathy for our kids.

Soren Kierkegaard wrote, "Prayer does not change God, but changes him who prays." A parent may be disappointed by his or her child's behavior from time to time. The disappointment may turn to personal hurt, especially if the parent's pride, reputation or expectations have been damaged by the child's behavior. Hurt often turns to anger, and anger often turns to depression. Through prayer and the Word of God, with the guidance and strengthening of the Holy Spirit, a parent is able to turn such a situation around by remaining tender-hearted and forgiving in his or her attitudes toward the child.

> *And be not conformed to this world: but be*
> *ye transformed by the renewing of your mind,*
> *that ye may prove what is that good, and accept-*
> *able, and perfect, will of God. (Rom. 12:2)*

Such a renewal process is ongoing in all of our lives. Through God's provisions and promises we learn how to overcome the temptation to take it personally when our child(ren) act in ways that disappoint us. We are given the grace to remember that we ourselves need forgiveness also, and such humility leads us to be kind, tender-hearted and forgiving toward our child(ren).

Your Children Are Your Reward

Lo, children are an heritage of the Lord: and the fruit of the womb is his reward. As arrows are in the hand of a mighty man; so are children of the youth. Happy is the man that hath his quiver full of them: they shall not be ashamed, but they shall speak with the enemies in the gate. (Ps. 127:3-5)

The person who is blessed with the gift of a child or children can claim his or her right to happiness because through the child(ren), God has rewarded the parent's faith. Some parents look upon their children as a burden, but the Christian parent knows that his or her child is a gift from God.

So much in life is contingent upon our view of things. How do you view your child(ren)? The way you view them comes across to the hearts of your children by way of your words, your examples and your attitudes.

Resentment is anger that is directed toward one's circumstances or toward other people. If permitted to fester, resentment will turn to bitterness. When this happens in families, many people are adversely affected:

*Looking diligently lest any man fail of the
grace of God; lest any root of bitterness springing up trouble you, and thereby many be defiled.
(Heb. 12:15)*

Financial problems, marital discord, losses and hurts
can all lead to bitterness in one's life. We are admonished
by the author of the Book of Hebrews to look diligently,
watching to be sure that no one (including ourselves) would
fail to appropriate God's grace for his circumstances.

The promise of God reminds parents that no situation
is too difficult for His grace to handle. Circumstances do
not have to be our master. Feelings are not our lord. No
matter what the difficulty may be, He speaks to your heart:

*My grace is sufficient for thee: for my
strength is made perfect in weakness. (2 Cor. 12:9)*

*And God is able to make all grace abound
toward you; that ye, always having all sufficiency in all things, may abound to every good
work. (2 Cor. 9:8)*

The Power of God's Word

The anchor that grips the solid Rock (Jesus), and
holds us secure in the storms and upheavals of life is the
Bible. It is our compass, our guidebook, our map, and our
rudder in all things, including parenting.

As Christian parents, it is our responsibility to show
the truth and power of God's Word to our children both by

teaching and by living. "Talking the talk" never works with kids unless we are also "walking the walk" in front of them.

If we want them to obey, we must be obedient. If we want them to pray, we must model a life of prayer. If we want them to be loving and kind, we must exhibit those attitudes. The Word of God is our standard — it is also a source of power that enables us to become more like Christ in all that we do.

> *And these words, which I command thee this day, shall be in thine heart: And thou shalt teach them diligently unto thy children, and shalt talk of them when thou sittest in thine house, and when thou walkest by the way* [or when you are driving in a car], *and when thou liest down, and when thou risest up. And thou shalt bind them for a sign upon thine hand, and they shall be as frontlets between thine eyes. And thou shalt write them upon the posts of thy house, and on thy gates. (Deut. 6:6-9)*

An old Sunday school chorus proclaims, "Every promise in the Book is mine." We need to remember this; we can claim and appropriate all the promises of God for our lives as parents and for the health, happiness and success of our children.

The Lord has announced: "Behold, I am the Lord, the God of all flesh: is there any thing too hard for me?" (Jer. 32:27). This rhetorical question requires no answer because we know "with God all things are possible" (Matt. 19:26).

Reach out and take hold of all that God has for you and your child(ren). The Bible will build your faith to enable you to take your loving heavenly Father at His Word. He cannot fail. You can build your life on the Bible. When you do so, you are able to focus on the promises of God rather than the problems of life. In your parenting, you become promise-centered rather than problem-centered. When problems come, you will take positive action rather than reacting out of fear, discouragement or anger.

Prayers That Prevail for Your Children takes this approach. As you meditate on and pray the Scripture-based prayers of this book, many things will change in your life and the lives of your children. Indeed, an exciting adventure of prevailing in prayer awaits you as you take hold of God's promises:

And he shall turn the heart of the fathers to the children, and the heart of the children to their fathers, lest I come and smite the earth with a curse. (Mal. 4:6)

Children's children are the crown of old men; and the glory of children are their fathers. (Prov. 17:6)

Correct thy son, and he shall give thee rest; yea, he shall give delight unto thy soul. (Prov. 29:17)

The father of the righteous shall greatly rejoice: and he that begetteth a wise child shall have joy of him. (Prov. 23:24)

And all thy children shall be taught of the Lord; and great shall be the peace of thy children. (Isa. 54:13)

Now unto him that is able to do exceeding abundantly above all that we ask or think, according to the power that worketh in us, Unto him be glory in the church by Christ Jesus throughout all ages, world without end. Amen. (Eph. 3:20-21)

BIBLICAL GOALS FOR PARENTS

A Parent's Greatest Resource

Being a parent in today's society is an awesome responsibility. It requires more skill and perseverance than any other role in life. Parenting is truly a ministry of eternal proportions.

Though it is hard work, parenting is immensely rewarding. It is a creative endeavor that involves the shaping and molding of a precious life. In this process, we become "labourers together with God" (1 Cor. 3:9) who is vitally concerned about the welfare of our child(ren).

We cannot become what parents should be without His help. As parents, we must learn to say with Paul, "I can do all things through Christ which strengtheneth me" (Phil. 4:13).

Jesus said, "I am the vine, ye are the branches: He that abideth in me, and I in him, the same bringeth forth much fruit; for without me ye can do nothing" (John 15:5). It is this exciting truth that every parent must recall and act on daily.

God has been so good to us. As our loving heavenly Father, He has made certain that all our needs have been supplied. In fact, He promises this to us in no uncertain words: "But my God shall supply all your need according to his riches in glory by Christ Jesus" (Phil. 4:19).

As we learn to appropriate God's promises into our sacred calling as parents, our faith is built up and our children are blessed. As in all things, Jesus has paved the way for us. He said, "I will pray the Father, and he shall give you another Comforter, that he may abide with you for ever; Even the Spirit of truth; whom the world cannot receive, because it seeth him not, neither knoweth him: but ye know him; for he dwelleth with you, and shall be in you" (John 14:16-17).

Every parent who understands and receives the truth of these words of Jesus has learned the secret to effective parenting. That secret is found as we open our hearts and our lives to the power and wisdom and truth of God's Holy Spirit. We are not alone. He dwells with us and He lives within us.

This is a parent's greatest resource — the power of God's Spirit who inhabits each believer's heart. The fruit of the Spirit's indwelling is "love, joy, peace, longsuffering, gentleness, goodness, faith, Meekness, temperance: against such there is no law" (Gal. 5:22-23).

The parent who bears such fruit in his/her dealings with his/her child(ren) is an effective parent. The child of such a parent reaches out to take the fruit of the Spirit for himself — to "taste and see that the Lord is good" (Ps. 34:8).

Through personal prayer — a daily quiet time — a parent draws close to Jesus, the Vine of Life. Workers in vineyards prune the branches of grapevines very close to the main vine in order to make them more fruitful. The closer we get to Jesus, through His Word, prayer and the presence of the Holy Spirit, the more fruitful we become in our parenting and in all the responsibilities and relationships of our lives.

Through prayer we learn how to abide in Him and to let His words abide in us. The result of such abiding is answered prayer: "If ye abide in me, and my words abide in you, ye shall ask what ye will, and it shall be done unto you" (John 15:7). Believing activates this promise in behalf of our children as we learn to abide in our Lord and Savior Jesus Christ.

By praying the Word of God, by using the topical prayers in *Prayers That Prevail for Your Children*, we become like the man described in Psalms 1:

> *Blessed is the man that walketh not in the counsel of the ungodly, nor standeth in the way of sinners, nor sitteth in the seat of the scornful. But his delight is in the law of the Lord* [the Word of God]*; and in his law doth he meditate day and night. And he shall be like a tree planted by the rivers of water, that bringeth forth his fruit in his season; his leaf also shall not wither; and whatsoever he doeth shall prosper.*

Praying the Word of God enables us to meditate upon His truths, His principles, His precepts. It gives us wisdom in living and in parenting. God promises that when we pray this way, He will give us stability. We will become like trees "planted by the rivers of water." These are healthy, strong trees that are not affected by floods, storms or winds; they stand fast and impart a sense of constancy and permanence to their environment. Parents with such stability give peace and security to their children.

The individual who meditates upon God's Word day and night will become fruitful in all his endeavors as well. This involves fruitfulness in every area of life, including the wonderful fruit of the Spirit that we previously outlined — the qualities of effective parenting that lead to happy, healthy children. The Spirit of God is present and active when we meditate upon the Word of God — the sword of the Spirit (Eph. 6:17).

Another benefit of meditating upon and praying God's Word (as outlined in Psalms 1) is prosperity. Whatever you do shall prosper. This includes, but goes well beyond, the dimension of financial prosperity, into the more important realm of spiritual prosperity and prosperity in our relationships with one another. It is the kind of prosperity that Paul shows us in a powerful prayer promise from Ephesians:

> *Now unto him that is able to do exceeding abundantly above all that we ask or think, according to the power that worketh in us, Unto him be glory in the church by Christ Jesus throughout all ages, world without end. Amen. (Eph. 3:20-21)*

The Power That Works Within Us

"Be filled with the Spirit" (Eph. 5:18), Paul admonished the young church at Ephesus. He was giving them the key to successful church life. It is also the key to a successful home life, as the succeeding verses of Ephesians 5 point out. This is "the power that worketh in us," (Eph. 3:20), and it is the power that enables us to be good parents as well.

Jesus said, "All power is given unto me in heaven and in earth" (Matt. 28:18). The One who has all power in the universe has created us to be the temples of His Spirit: "What? know ye not that your body is the temple of the Holy Ghost which is in you, which ye have of God, and ye are not your own? For ye are bought with a price: therefore glorify God in your body, and in your spirit, which are God's" (1 Cor. 6:19-20).

The power that enables a parent to pursue biblical goals that God has instituted for children is also the power that enables parents and children to fulfill the goals. That dynamic resource is actualized through prayer.

Prayer Power

The mother of John and Charles Wesley, Susanna, had nineteen children (of whom eight died as infants). She made a faithful practice of spending at least one hour per week with each child separately, listening to them, praying for them and teaching them God's Word. The result? Revival in the British Isles. (To learn more about the exciting, inspirational effect of parental prayers in the lives of the Wesleys, Jonathan Edwards and others, be sure to read the next section of this book entitled, "The Living Legacy of Godly Parents.")

The power of prayer is lasting. It is a stream of divine energy that flows to each generation, carrying with it the grace and goodness of God.

Through believing prayer, based upon the promises and principles of God's Word, the Christian parent unleashes the power of God's Spirit to effect positive changes in the lives of his or her children. Dramatic, lasting changes are the wonderful result. As Andrew Murray points out, "The faith in God's Word can nowhere be so exercised and perfected as in the intercession that asks, expects, and looks out for the answer. Throughout Scripture, in the life of every saint, of God's own Son, throughout the history of God's Church, God is, first of all, a prayer-hearing God. Let us try and help God's children to know their God, and encourage all God's servants to labor with the assurance: the chief and most blessed part of my work is to ask and receive from my Father what I can bring to others" (From *The Ministry of Intercession* by Andrew Murray.)

An amazing adventure awaits every parent who will put God's Word into action by way of intercessory prayer in behalf of his or her children. When we ask the Father, we shall receive, and in the process, both our children and we ourselves will be changed.

Ten Keys to Good Parenting

1. *God wants every member of your family to be saved.* Pray for the salvation of your children. God wants them to receive Jesus Christ as their personal Lord and Savior, and He will answer your prayers for their salvation if you show them *at home* that the Christian life is the greatest life of all.

> *And they said, Believe on the Lord Jesus Christ, and thou shalt be saved, and thy house. (Acts 16:31)*

2. *God wants you to model your Christian commitment in front of your children.* Christianity is "caught," not just taught. By living a godly life before our children, we ensure that they will see the practical truth of the Gospel of Jesus Christ demonstrated. This is an important ingredient in effective intercessory prayer for our children; we need to live our prayers as well as speak them.

> *And if it seem evil unto you to serve the Lord, choose you this day whom ye will serve; whether the gods which your fathers served that were on the other side of the flood, or the gods of the Amorites, in whose land ye dwell: but as for me and my house, we will serve the Lord. (Josh. 24:15)*

3. *Forgiveness leads to trust in all family relationships.* Forgiveness, acceptance and unconditional love are all closely related; they are integral components in all good relationships, especially those within the family setting. Caring parent-child relationships involve forgiveness. When we, as parents, seek our child's forgiveness when we make mistakes that affect him or her, we show him or her that we have the same human needs he or she does, that we respect him or her and that we want him or her to be emotionally healthy.

*Let all bitterness, and wrath, and anger,
and clamour, and evil speaking, be put away
from you, with all malice: And be ye kind one to
another, tenderhearted, forgiving one another,
even as God for Christ's sake hath forgiven you.
(Eph. 4:31-32)*

4. *Christian training for our children.* We train our children through example, teaching, prayer and counseling. The core dimensions of such training include: trust, warmth, genuineness, empathy and love. It is always important for parents to remember back to their own childhoods in an effort to understand their child's behaviors and feelings, not to issue pronouncements such as: "When I was a child...." In such a caring and nurturing atmosphere, the Word of God can be imparted to the hearts of our children with success. Children in a caring Christian environment become fertile soil for the implanting of seeds from God's Word.

*Train up a child in the way he should go:
and when he is old, he will not depart from it.
(Prov. 22:6)*

5. *Respect for one another.* In order to gain respect from one's children, the godly parent must exhibit respect for his or her children. Our children will honor us if we honor them. A slogan popularized by one television commercial provides a wise piece of advice for parents today: "Treat family like company and company like family." All too often we treat company like company and family members like things.

*Honour thy father and thy mother: that thy
days may be long upon the land which the Lord
thy God giveth thee. (Exod. 20:12)*

*Provoke not your children to wrath: but
bring them up in the nurture and admonition of
the Lord. (Eph. 6:4)*

6. *Godly leadership produces solid Christians.* A
good leader (parent) persuades people by way of positive
reinforcement, good example, reason and by appealing to
all that is good and strong within the individual. A good
leader motivates people by kind, understanding leadership, never by forceful manipulation. A Christian parent
is most effective when he or she is able to gently guide his
or her children rather than pushing them.

*The God of Israel spoke, the Rock of Israel
said to me: When one rules over men in righteousness, when he rules in the fear of God, he is
like the light of morning at sunrise on a cloud-
less morning, like the brightness after rain that
brings the grass from the earth. "Is not my
house right with God? Has he not made with me
an everlasting covenant, arranged and secured
in every part? Will he not bring to fruition my
salvation and grant me my every desire?" (2
Sam 23:3-5).*

7. *Showing our children that we highly value them.*
Daily, we need to demonstrate to our children that they are
worth very much to us. We do this by giving as many positive affirmations to each child as possible. We need to
train ourselves to praise their virtues and strengths instead

of focusing on their weaknesses. At all times, we must let each child know that he or she is an important, vital part of the family.

> *Lo, children are an heritage of the Lord: and the fruit of the womb is his reward. As arrows are in the hand of a mighty man; so are children of the youth. Happy is the man that hath his quiver full of them: they shall not be ashamed, but they shall speak with the enemies in the gate. (Ps. 127:3-5)*

8. *Building a relationship with our children.* In the same way that Christianity is a relationship, not a religion, the Christian family is a home built by relationships, not just a house made of building materials. Relationships are developed through good communication, including the all-important communication with God through prayer. Communication skills include active listening (going beneath the surface, listening for the feelings of the heart as well as the words), touch, eye-to-eye contact ("I will guide thee with mine eye" — Ps. 32:8), and attention to the needs of others.

> *And he shall turn the heart of the fathers to the children, and the heart of the children to their fathers, lest I come and smite the earth with a curse. (Mal. 4:6)*

9. *Teaching Christian values.* A good teacher is enthusiastic about his or her subject. He or she loves the students under his or her care, and he or she also loves to learn and to teach. To be a good teacher to our children, therefore, we need to join with them in the learning process, to show them that the Christian life is an exciting adventure and to lead them into the principles, precepts and promises of God's Word.

> *And these words, which I command thee this day, shall be in thine heart: And thou shalt teach them diligently unto thy children, and shalt talk of them when thou sittest in thine house, and when thou walkest by the way, and when thou liest down, and when thou risest up. And thou shalt bind them for a sign upon thine hand, and they shall be as frontlets between thine eyes. And thou shalt write them upon the posts of thy house, and on thy gates. (Deut. 6:6-9)*

10. *Discipline.* Discipline involves more than punishment, correction and chastisement. More important than any of these elements, are training, shaping, molding and preparing a life for Christian service. This is the goal of Christian parenting — to lead our children to become disciples of the Lord Jesus Christ.

> *Correct thy son, and he shall give thee rest; yea, he shall give delight unto thy soul. (Prov. 29:17)*

Good discipline is administered consistently so that the child will have the security of always knowing what to expect.

Promises That Prevail

When each of the ten keys to good parenting are put into use, the Christian parent has an assurance that his or her prayers will be heard and answered by our loving heavenly Father. The promises of His Word cannot fail.

> *Blessed is every one that feareth the Lord; that walketh in his ways. For thou shalt eat the labour of thine hands: happy shalt thou be, and it shall be well with thee. Thy wife shall be as a fruitful vine by the sides of thine house: thy children like olive plants round about thy table. Behold, that thus shall the man be blessed that feareth the Lord. (Ps. 128:1-4)*

> *The father of the righteous shall greatly rejoice: and he that begetteth a wise child shall have joy of him. (Prov. 23:24)*

> *And all thy children shall be taught of the Lord; and great shall be the peace of thy children. (Isa. 54:13)*

THE LIVING LEGACY OF GODLY PARENTS

Praying for our children is a primary parental responsibility. More profoundly, it is a ministry of eternal proportions. Through prayer, we make an investment in the lives of our children that will pay rich dividends in their futures, the lives of their children and in all succeeding generations. The far-reaching impact of our believing prayers will influence countless others as well.

Take, for example, what happened in the life of Samuel, an Old Testament prophet (eleventh century B.C.) who anointed Saul and David as kings over Israel. He was known as "the child of prayer," because Hannah (his mother) had prayed for him:

> *For this child I prayed; and the Lord hath given me my petition which I asked of him: Therefore also I have lent him to the Lord. (1 Sam. 1:27-28)*

E.M. Bounds writes about the power of Hannah's prayers: "Samuel came into this world and was given existence in direct answer to prayer. He was born of a praying mother, whose heart was full of earnest desire for a son. He came into life under prayer surroundings, and his first months in this world were spent in direct contact with a woman who knew how to pray. It was a prayer accompanied by a solemn vow that if he should be given, he should be 'lent unto the Lord,' and true to that vow, this praying mother put him directly in touch with the minister of the sanctuary and under the influence of the 'house of prayer.' It was no wonder he developed into a man of prayer. We could not have expected otherwise with such a beginning in life and with such early environments. Such surroundings always make impressions upon children and tend to make character and determine destiny."

Samuel was affected by Hannah's praying both supernaturally and naturally. Her prayers for the son she lent to the Lord were heard and answered by a loving God in dramatic ways, and by observing Hannah's godly example in prayer, Samuel learned the importance of prayer for his own life.

The praying saints of the Old and New Testaments gave great priority to prayer for their children. The results of their faith-filled prayers were explosive, and they continue to affect and influence people's lives even now, centuries after their prayers were expressed to God.

Parents who pray for their children soon learn that prayer is their greatest resource in parenting. When their child is ill, disobedient or frightened, prayer applies the healing Balm of Gilead to their bodies and souls. By blending their faith with the Word of God as they lift their children up in prayer, Christian parents discover what God wants them to do and how He wants them to do it. All He expects of them is faith in His Word, obedience to His teaching and the investment of their time in the exciting and wondrous life of prayer.

When the Apostle Paul wrote to his son-in-the-faith, Timothy, he recalled the unfeigned (sincere) faith of Timothy's mother, Eunice, and his grandmother, Lois. Like Samuel, Timothy had a praying mother who believed God in behalf of her son and appropriated the promises of God's Word for his life. Children who grow up with such spiritual support become tools the Master can use.

> *I call to remembrance the unfeigned faith that is in thee, which dwelt first in thy grandmother Lois, and thy mother Eunice; and I am persuaded that in thee also. (2 Tim. 1:5)*

The importance of the prayers and righteous examples of godly parents and grandparents must never be discounted or minimized. The Bible and Church history are replete with examples of men and women who were trained for service in God's army by committed Christian parents who loved them and prayed for them regularly. The effects of those parents' prayers live on from generation to generation. These parents of prayer are like Abraham, of whom it was said, "He being dead, yet speaketh" (Heb. 11:4). The power of their prayers will always live.

When young people excel in Olympic competitions and other endeavors, little thought may be given to their parents who invested so much of themselves, sometimes sacrificially, to ensure the success of their children. The same may be true in the spiritual dimension. Parents have the wonderful responsibility of being co-laborers with God in the nurture and training of their children. Prayerful, godly parents deserve recognition in God's Hall of Fame of Faith. The following vignettes (glimpses into the lives of some of these godly parents and their progeny) show how the prayers of parents result in lasting blessings.

Jonathan and Sarah Edwards

The Edwardses had eleven children. Before dawn each morning, Jonathan would wake his children for morning prayer by candlelight. He would read a chapter from the Bible and then pray God's blessing on each of the children, the family and the day ahead.

These prayers had lasting effects. By the turn of the twentieth century, the sacred union of Jonathan and Sarah Edwards (eighteenth century) had produced thirteen college presidents, sixty-five professors, 100 lawyers (including a dean of a law school), thirty judges, fifty-six physicians, a medical-school dean, eighty public-office holders, three U.S. Senators, three mayors of large American cities, three governors, one Vice President of the United States, and one comptroller of the U.S. Treasury. In addition, 100 family members became over-seas missionaries, and several descendants of the Edwardses wrote books and articles (135 books in all).

Timothy Dwight, one of the Edwards's grandsons, was the President of Yale University in 1802. Revival broke forth as he preached at the university chapel services and approximately one-third of the students were converted to Christ. Two of the students, Lyman Beecher and Nathaniel Taylor, became leaders in the Second Great Awakening Revival in America which began in the 1820's.

Without question, Jonathan Edwards knew the power of prayer. Through careful preparation in prayer, Rev.

Edwards brought to birth the Great Awakening in America, a revival that touched every community with the Gospel of Jesus Christ. (Not coincidentally, Jonathan was the son of a Congregational pastor who had surely spent much time in prayer for his son.)

Following in Jonathan's footsteps was George Whitefield (1714-1770), who greatly reinforced the Great Awakening. Prayer — the strength and preparation for our children, and the key to revival!

Joseph and Mary

We would be remiss in not including the parents of our Lord and Savior Jesus Christ in this section because Mary and Joseph are pristine examples of godly parents who knew the power of prayer. When the angel told Mary that she had been chosen to bear the Son of God, she turned to her heavenly Father in prayer:

> *My soul doth magnify the Lord. And my spirit hath rejoiced in God my Saviour. For he hath regarded the low estate of his handmaiden: for, behold, from henceforth all generations shall call me blessed. For he that is mighty hath done to me great things; and holy is his name. And his mercy is on them that fear him from generation to generation. He hath shewed strength with his arm; he hath scattered the proud in the imagination of their hearts. He hath put down the mighty from their seats, and exalted them of low degree. He hath filled the hungry with good things; and the rich he hath*

sent empty away. He hath holpen his servant
Israel, in remembrance of his mercy; As he
spake to our fathers, to Abraham, and to his
seed for ever. (Luke 1:46-55)

Mary knew God. She loved Him, and she purposed
in her heart to serve Him forever. Along with her husband,
Joseph, Mary spent much time in prayer and worship.
Their precious son, Jesus, wanted to be about His Father's
business when He was only twelve years of age. Instead,
however, He obeyed His earthly parents by returning to
Nazareth with them. In the atmosphere of their modest
home, Jesus learned about the things of God,

And Jesus increased in wisdom and stature,
and in favour with God and man. (Luke 2:52)

Susanna Wesley

The mother of John and Charles Wesley, Susanna,
had nineteen children (of whom eight died as infants).
Her faithful practice was to spend at least one hour per
week with each child separately, listening to them,
praying for them and teaching them God's Word.
Susanna's prayers, like those of the woman who bore her
name in the Gospel of Luke, were based on love for the
Lord and faith in His Word.

She claimed the promises of God in behalf of her
children, and He heard her earnest pleas. The Lord moved
and answered in marvelous and unexpected ways.

John Wesley became the most famous leader of the
Evangelical movement in the British Isles, the founder of

Methodism. All this occurred as a result of his parents' prayers for his salvation. It must have brought great rejoicing to the hearts of his parents (Samuel and Susanna) when John experienced what he recorded in his diary on May 24, 1738:

> *About a quarter before nine, while he* [Luther's preface to the Book of Romans] *was describing the change which God works in the heart through faith in Christ, I felt my heart strangely warmed. I felt I did trust in Christ, Christ alone, for salvation; and an assurance was given me that he had taken away my sins, even mine, and saved me from the law of sin and death.*

Wesley's radical conversion is known as his Aldersgate experience because he was attending an Anglican Society meeting on Aldersgate Street in London when God broke through to him, and his heart was "strangely warmed." Along with George Whitefield, John and Charles Wesley served God as missionaries to America and revivalists throughout the British Isles. John Wesley stated, "The world is my parish," and indeed it was so. In many ways, it remains his parish today. John translated numerous German hymns into English, and Charles composed great hymns of the Church that are sung the world over still today. Some of Charles's best-known hymns include: "Jesus, Lover of My Soul," "Love Divine, All Loves Excelling," "O, for a Thousand Tongues to Sing," and "Christ, the Lord, Is Risen Today."

Thank you, Samuel and Susanna Wesley, for your faithfulness in prayer and godly parenting.

James and Mary Liddell

The parents of Eric Liddell, Olympic champion and missionary to China, belonged to a strict Evangelical tradition. They loved the gospel hymns of D.L. Moody and Ira Sankey, and they sang these choruses to their four children. Missionaries to China themselves, they knew the power of prayer. Each day they asked God to bless and guide their children.

When James and Mary went to China as Scottish Presbyterian missionaries, they left two of their children (Eric and Rob) in Scotland. The boys attended a Christian school that served many children of foreign missionaries. As often as possible, Mary was faithful to write regular letters of spiritual encouragement to her sons who were thousands of miles away from her, and these letters reveal that she carried them in her heart, praying for them regularly. The godly example, love and prayers of James and Mary Liddell were heard and answered by their heavenly Father.

As Russell Ramsey wrote, "Eric Liddell was God's gentle knight. He was the perfect example of the Olympic amateur athlete. He was a serious, powerful theologian, and he practiced a vigorous, committed Christian life....Eric Liddell promises deepest joy from the belief and practice of Christian love unending. He invites us all to become gentle knights, to experience the thrill of breaking the tape as God's joyful runner."

Ramsey writes of Eric as if his subject were still alive. It is appropriate for him to do so because Eric's witness lives on in the form of books, memories and the Academy-Award-winning film about his life, "Chariots of Fire."

Likewise, the legacy of James and Mary Liddell lives on. God rewarded their faithfulness in surprising ways. As missionaries to China before World War II, it is unlikely that they would ever have imagined that one day their son's obedience to God would give him an enduring world-wide witness. They knew, however, the truth of God's Word:

Now unto him that is able to do exceeding abundantly above all that we ask or think, according to the power that worketh in us, Unto him be glory in the church by Christ Jesus throughout all ages, world without end. (Eph. 3:20-21)

George and Helen MacDonald

Though George MacDonald Jr.'s godly mother, Helen, died when he was eight (due to tuberculosis), his father, George, Sr., continued to hold forth the standard of God's love in front of his son. The elder MacDonald was later described by his pastor-writer son as a brave, patient and generous man who had profound insights into the love of God. Obviously, these godly qualities impressed the young boy, and surely he related these attributes of his earthly father to those of his heavenly Father.

George MacDonald's father was a deacon in his Scottish Congregational church. Every Monday morning the father would visit with the church's minister for prayer and fellowship. Together, the deacon and the pastor would pray for the MacDonald boys.

About George MacDonald, Jr., C.S. Lewis wrote, "I regarded him as my master." Lewis described the young MacDonald's relationship with his earthly father thusly: "An almost perfect relationship with his father was the earthly root of all his wisdom. From his own father, he said, he first learned that Fatherhood must be at the core of the universe. He was thus prepared in an unusual way to teach that religion in which the relation of Father and Son is of all relations the most central."

George MacDonald, as a result of his relationship with his loving father, became a preacher, poet, scholar, novelist, teacher and apologist for the faith. His works continue to influence young and old today. Many Christian parents read MacDonald's fantasy novel, *At the Back of the North Wind*, to their children as a delightful allegory that teaches Christian truths. Had not Helen and George MacDonald prayed for their son and lived a Christian life in front of him, the world might not have been able to read his books or the books of his twentieth-century prodigy, C.S. Lewis. (The blessing continues. One of Lewis's greatest works of Christian apologetics, *Mere Christianity*, remains on the best-seller charts today, leading countless readers to a saving knowledge of Jesus Christ.)

John Spurgeon

The father of Charles Haddon Spurgeon, John, and his grandfather, James, were Nonconformist ministers in Victorian England. Charles's mother had seventeen children, of whom nine died in infancy. The young Spurgeon recalls that his earliest memories of childhood involved listening to sermons, learning hymns and looking at pictures in *The Pilgrim's Progress* and *Foxe's Book of Martyrs*. His father, his grandparents and his aunt taught him to pray and read the Bible daily, as they themselves did. In such a godly environment, Spurgeon learned the value of prayer, and the prayers of those who loved him were mightily answered.

Through most of the nineteenth century, Spurgeon was known as "The Prince of Preachers." He greatly influenced the Baptist and Evangelical movements. He did far more than preaching; he founded lasting homes for orphans, much like his contemporary, George Muller.

Charles Haddon Spurgeon — the product of the believing prayers of his father and mother, his grandparents and other committed Christians in his extended family.

Hidden Heroes of Prayer

In millions of homes around the world, Christian parents are faithfully praying for their children. They reach out and take hold of God's promises for their children. They believe God, and it is counted unto them as righteousness. Not all of their children grow up to be famous preachers like Moody, Spurgeon, Wesley and Edwards. Not all of them become writers like George MacDonald and C.S Lewis. One thing is certain, however, the children of these praying parents learn to know God and serve Him. Some become pastors, choir members, Sunday school teachers or Christian workers; others serve more quietly in their given spheres. Most, however, do become parents — praying parents — and the blessings their parents prayed over them become a stream of God's power to all the lineage of the family.

When we offer our children as gifts from God that we are dedicating to Him, amazing things begin to happen. Our children change before our eyes. Our attitudes toward our children change. God is free to work in their lives.

In the same way that Moses and Aaron would offer burnt offerings to God on the altar of sacrifice every morning, we need to place the lives of our children before Him. We need to remember that God always takes good care of His property. Our children are on loan to us so that we can help to instruct them in righteousness. Our prayers for them become like the fire that burns on the Old Testament altar of sacrifice:

> *The fire shall ever be burning upon the altar; it shall never go out. (Lev. 6:13)*

When we pray for our children we must believe that the light and fire of God in their lives will never go out, that it will guide them into all truth. Such faith will be rewarded.

As Smith Wigglesworth has observed, "Faith is the audacity that rejoices in the fact that God cannot break His own Word. Faith is not agitation; it is quiet confidence that God means what He says, and we act on His Word."

PRAYERS FOR YOUR CHILDREN

Abiding in Christ

Key Thought: Abiding in Christ leads to answered prayer.

Key Scripture: *"Abide in me, and I in you. As the branch cannot bear fruit of itself, except it abide in the vine; no more can ye, except ye abide in me. I am the vine, ye are the branches: He that abideth in me, and I in him, the same bringeth forth much fruit: for without me ye can do nothing" (John 15:4-5).*

Prayer: Heavenly Father, teach my son/daughter, _____ _____ , to abide in you constantly. Reveal to him/her that if he/she will abide in you, and let your words abide in him/her, that he/she will be able to ask whatever he/she wills, and it shall be done for him/her.[1] Let _____ know that abiding in you will keep him/her from sin[2] and make him/her fruitful in your kingdom.[3] Teach him/her to abide — to settle, dwell, take root, live — in you.

You, Lord, are the vine. I pray that the life of _____ _____ will always be a branch in your vine. May his/her life always stem from you. Graft him/her into your vine, and prune his/her life of all things that do not lead to growth and fruitfulness.[4]

May my son/daughter realize early, Lord, that apart from you, he/she can accomplish nothing,[3] but through you, he/she can do all things.[5]

I pray that he/she will always endeavor to obey your command to love others[6] and experience abiding in your love.[7]

Thank you, Father, for being a refuge and fortress for _____. May he/she ever trust in you as he/she abides under your shadow and dwells in the secret place of your presence.[8] Thank you for sending your Holy Spirit to _____; may He ever abide with him/her.[9] Show my child the secret of abiding in your great love, O Father.[10]

I pray that _____ will always remember that you have bought him/her with a tremendous price, and that it is his/her responsibility to serve you first, before others.[11] Thank you for calling him/her.

Impart to him/her the anointing of your Holy Spirit. I pray, O Lord, that that same anointing would abide in him/her, teaching him/her your will, your ways and your truth. Because of your abiding presence in the life of _____, he/she will have no reason to be ashamed at your coming.[12]

References: (1) John 15:7; (2) 1 John 3:6; (3) John 15:5; (4) John 15:1,2; (5) Philippians 4:13; (6) John 15:12; (7) John 15:10; (8) Psalms 91:1; (9) John 14:16; (10) 1 John 3:24; (11) 1 Corinthians 7:23; (12) 1 John 2:27,28.

Achievement

Key Thought: Achievement in God's eyes is far different from the way society views achievement.

Key Scripture: *"Except the Lord build the house, they labour in vain that build it: except the Lord keep the city, the watchman waketh but in vain" (Ps. 127:1).*

Prayer: Lord God, help my son/daughter, _____
_____, to grow in the grace and knowledge of our Lord and Savior Jesus Christ.[1] Help him/her to understand early in life that true success is a matter of yielding one's heart, soul and life to you. Lead him/her to know that through wisdom a house is built, and by understanding it is established.[2]

Reveal to him/her that all the wisdom he/she needs for successful living is found in Jesus Christ,[3] the living Word,[4] and is available to anyone who asks with a believing heart.[5]

Give grace to my son/daughter, Lord, that would enable him/her to know that a good name is better than precious ointment,[6] and it is wonderful for a person to be able to rejoice in his/her own works.[7]

Your Son, our Lord Jesus Christ, proclaimed that a person would be known by his/her fruits.[8] Lord, I ask that you would develop fruitfulness in the life of my son/daughter; may he/she ever produce the fruit of your Spirit — love, peace, joy, patience, meekness, gentleness, faithfulness, goodness and self-control.[9]

Help him/her to know that without Jesus he/she can do nothing,[10] but that through Him he/she can do all things.[11] May his/her constant motivation be to do all for your glory,[12] so that at the end of his/her life he/she will be able to proclaim, "I have fought a good fight, I have finished my course, I have kept the faith".[13] This, Lord, is true success and achievement.

You are the Potter; we are the clay.[14] Shape and mold my child in your hands, Lord, until he/she would be conformed to the image of your Son.[15] I thank you that he/she is your workmanship in Christ Jesus,[16] and I know that you will continue your workmanship throughout his/her life.[17] Thank you, Father.

You have built all things, Lord.[18] You are the Author and Finisher of our faith, and I ask you to give my son/daughter the capacity of keeping his/her focus on you so that he/she will be able to keep running the race with persistence.[19]

How I praise you, mighty Lord, that nothing shall be able to separate my son/daughter from your love in Jesus Christ.[20]

References: *(1) 2 Peter 3:18; (2) Proverbs 24:3; (3) 1 Corinthians 1:23-30; (4) John 1:14; (5) James 1:5-6; (6) Ecclesiastes 7:1; (7) Ecclesiastes 3:22; (8) Matthew 7:20; (9) Galatians 5:22-23; (10) John 15:5; (11) Philippians 4:13; (12) 1 Corinthians 10:31; (13) 2 Timothy 4:7; (14) Isaiah 64:8; (15) Romans 8:29; (16) Ephesians 2:10; (17) Philippians 1:6; (18) Hebrews 3:4; (19) Hebrews 12:2; (20) Romans 8:38-39.*

The Addicted Child

Key Thought: The Bible is God's Emancipation Proclamation for everyone who is in bondage.

Key Scripture: *"Stand fast therefore in the liberty wherewith Christ hath made us free, and be not entangled again with the yoke of bondage" (Gal. 5:1).* Claim this promise for your son/daughter.

Prayer: Lord God, thank you for sending Jesus who preached the gospel to the poor, healed the brokenhearted, preached deliverance to the captives and recovering of sight to the blind.[1] I pray that you will deliver my son/daughter, _____, from his/her addiction to _____.[2] Set him/her free from his/her captivity.[3] The promises of your Word give great comfort to me, Lord. All your promises are yes in Christ,[4] and I know you hear my prayer,[5] and I know you will answer me according to your Word.[6] Thank you, Lord, for the wonderful assurance I have in you.

You have promised to set at liberty those who are bruised.[7] Set _____ free. Heal his/her bruises and bind up his/her broken heart.[8] I know that you will never break a reed that is bruised.[9] Thank you for your tender, loving care[10] in the life of my son/daughter, and thank you for bringing healing to him/her.[11]

Reveal to _____ that you meet all the needs of the human heart,[12] that it is not your will for him/her to be in bondage to anything, and that you are Almighty God, the only one who can restore hope,[13] joy,[14] purpose,[15] and abundant life[16] to him/her. Father, bring salvation to my son/daughter.[17] Let him/her know how much you love him/her.[18] I pray that he/she will come to a saving knowledge of your Son, the Lord Jesus Christ.[19] Grant _____ repentance[20] so that he/she will turn to you with all his/her heart,[21] acknowledge you as his/her Savior and Lord,[22] and begin life all over again as a new creation in you.[23] Cleanse him/her from all his/her sins as he/she turns his/her life over to you in complete surrender.[24] Give him/her the willingness to face the truth about his/her life, realizing that by so doing, the truth will make him/her free.[25]

Keep him/her in the hollow of your hand, Lord.[26] May he/she ever be the apple of your eye.[27] Give him/her the grace to always stand fast in the liberty by which you are setting him/her free, and may he/she never again be entangled with a yoke of bondage to any addiction.[28] I believe that even now you are answering this prayer, and I praise you for the certain knowledge that all those you set free are free indeed.[29]

References: *(1) Luke 4:18; (2) Psalms 59:1; (3) Zephaniah 2:7; (4) 2 Corinthians 1:20; (5) Jeremiah 33:3; (6) Matthew 7:7; (7) Luke 4:18; (8) Isaiah 61:1; (9) Isaiah 42:3; (10) 1 Peter 5:7; (11) Exodus 15:26; (12) Philippians 4:19; (13) Romans*

8:24; (14) Nehemiah 8:10; (15) Romans 8:28; (16) John 10:10; (17) Romans 10:9-10; (18) John 3:16; (19) Matthew 18:11; (20) Acts 8:22; (21) Malachi 3:7; (22) Ephesians 4:5; (23) 2 Corinthians 5:17; (24) 1 John 1:9; (25) John 8:32; (26) John 10:28; (27) Deuteronomy 32:10; (28) Galatians 5:1; (29) John 8:36.

Angelic Protection

Key Thought: Angels guard and minister to our children.

Key Scripture: *"He shall give his angels charge concerning thee: and in their hands they shall bear thee up, lest at any time thou dash thy foot against a stone" (Matt. 4:6).*

Prayer: Thank you, Father, for the angelic host who minister to your people. In your heavenly realm there are thousands of chariots and tens of thousands of angels;[1] I pray that you will assign angels to protect my son/daughter, _____, throughout his/her life. Lord, I beseech you to let no evil befall my son/daughter as you give your angels charge over him/her, to keep him/her in all your ways.[2]

As your angels ministered so faithfully to our Lord Jesus, I pray that they will minister to my son/daughter at all times.[3] I thank you, Father, for the wonderful realization that angels who protect _____ are continually beholding your face in heaven.[4] Make him/her aware of the innumerable company of angels that are working in his/her behalf.[5]

Hasten the day, Lord, when Jesus shall send forth His angels to gather all things that offend out of His Kingdom, including all those who work iniquity.[6] I look forward to the time when your angels shall sever the wicked from

among the just.[7]   May my son/daughter always be
conscious of your power to defeat sin and may he/she
always choose to be counted among those who are the just.

Help _____ to know
that whoever will be ashamed of you and your Word in
this adulterous and sinful generation will be people of
whom your Son will be ashamed when He comes in your
glory with all the holy angels.[8] I pray that the desire of
his/her heart will always be to please you and may he/she
never bring dishonor to your name.

May the angel of the Lord encamp around _____
_____ , and deliver him/her as he/she
honors you with reverent fear, awe and respect.[9]

Thank you for sending your Son, our Lord and
Savior Jesus Christ, who speaks to us in these last days.
Thank you for giving Him power that is far greater than
angelic power and a name that is more excellent than the
names of angels.[10] Even so, I thank you, Father, that you
have made the angels to be ministering spirits who
worship you and whom you send to serve your people.
Thank you, Lord, for those angels who minister for the
heirs of salvation.[11]

References: *(1) Psalms 68:17; (2) Psalms 91:11; (3) Matthew
4:11; (4) Matthew 18:10; (5) Hebrews 12:22; (6) Matthew
13:41; (7) Matthew 13:49; (8) Matthew 25:31; (9) Psalms
34:7; (10) Hebrews 1:4; (11) Hebrews 1:6-7,14.*

An Angry Child

Key Thought: Anger is a symptom of hurt or frustration.

Key Scripture: *"The wrath of man worketh not the righteousness of God" (James 1:20).*

Prayer: Heavenly Father, thank you for my son/daughter, _____. Guide me at all times so that I will never provoke him/her to wrath;[1] instead, I want to be a support to him/her, a source of encouragement at all times in his/her life.[2]

So work in his/her life that he/she will soon realize that you are the Healer of all his/her inner hurts, frustrations, and disappointments.[3] Bind up all his/her wounds, Lord, and set him/her free from all his/her hurts that cause him/her to feel angry.[4] Allow me to be an agent of healing in his/her life at all times; please give me the wisdom I need to deal with him/her and his/her anger in healing and constructive ways.[5]

Father, I thank you for Jesus, our High Priest, who was tempted in all the ways that humans are tempted, yet without sin. I know that He understands why _____ _____ feels angry, and because this is so, I know that He will set him/her free.[6] Thank you for this promise which I now claim in behalf of my son/daughter.

Lord God, you are full of mercy and grace.[7] I ask you to apply your mercy and grace to the heart of my child; let your Balm of Gilead heal him/her of all hurts.[8] I pray that my son/daughter will learn that his/her anger is useful in that it will lead him/her to seek the help he/she needs from you. As he/she feels this anger, may he/she act upon it only in positive ways, always without sin.[9]

I pray that _____ will learn to cease from his/her anger and to forsake his/her wrath,[10] as he/she responds to your wonderful love in his/her life.[11] Reveal to him/her what the cause of his/her anger is, and help him/her to acknowledge the truth about his/her life because I know the truth will make him/her free.[12]

Lord, grant to my son/daughter the special ability to forgive any and all who may have hurt him/her.[13] Show _____ that any unresolved anger and/or unforgiveness in his/her heart is more damaging to him/her than it is to the ones to whom it is directed.[14] Give him/her the wisdom to identify and respond to his/her anger in healing ways.[15] I thank you for the certain knowledge that your justice will always prevail, and I ask you to lead my child to this understanding as well.[16]

Whenever anger becomes the experience of my son/daughter, Lord, I pray that he/she will be able to remember your mercy and his/her need to receive and reflect your mercy.[17] Help him/her to deal with his/her anger in positive ways, never permitting the sun to go down upon his/her wrath.[18] Teach him/her your perfect way in all things,[19] and help him/her to see that love is always the more excellent way.[20]

References: *(1) Ephesians 6:4; (2) Isaiah 41:6; (3) Exodus 15:26;
(4) Luke 4:18; (5) James 1:5; (6) Hebrews 4:15; (7) Psalms 86:5;
(8) Jeremiah 8:22; (9) Ephesians 4:26; (10) Psalms 37:8; (11) 1 John
4:10; (12) John 8:32; (13) Colossians 3:13; (14) Matthew 5:22;
(15) James 1:5; (16) Isaiah 61:8; (17) Habakkuk 3:2; (18) Ephesians
4:26; (19) Psalms 86:11; (20) 1 Corinthians 12:32.*

Attitude

Key Thought: The Beatitudes show what our attitudes should be.

Key Scripture: *"Therefore whosoever heareth these sayings of mine, and doeth them, I will liken him unto a wise man, which built his house upon a rock: And the rain descended, and the floods came, and the winds blew, and beat upon that house; and it fell not: for it was founded upon a rock" (Matt. 7:24-25).*

Prayer: Heavenly Father, your Word renews our minds,[1] and prayer changes the attitudes of our hearts. Teach _____ your ways, Father; reveal to him/her that your way is always perfect. You are a mighty buckler to all those who trust in you.[2] Lead _____ _____ to always trust in you instead of leaning to his/her own understanding. I pray that he/she will acknowledge you in all his/her ways, and I know that as he/she learns to do so, you will direct his/her paths.[3]

May his/her heart always be right before you, Father.[4] Search him/her, and see if there be any wrong attitudes in him/her.[5] Cleanse him/her of all unrighteousness as him/her learns to confess his/her wrong attitudes to you.[6] Help him/her to rise above any temptation to become resentful or bitter.[7]

Give him/her a great desire to serve you in newness of spirit, not in the oldness of the letter.[8] Shape his/her life in such a way that he/she will be tender-hearted, always willing to forgive those who wrong him/her, and to do so as often as necessary.[9] God, I pray that you will so work in the life of _____ that he/she will both will and do your good pleasure[10] at all times by being respectful,[11] kind,[12] caring,[13] merciful,[14] and helpful.[15] Teach _____ how to bless those who curse him/her, to love his/her enemies, to do good to those who hate him/her, and to pray for those who despitefully use him/her and say all manner of evil against him/her.[16] May he/she rarely encounter such individuals throughout his/her life.

Whenever _____ sees a fellow-believer overtaken in a fault, I pray that his/her response would be to restore such a one in the spirit of meekness, realizing his/her own vulnerabilities.[17] May your love be shed abroad in the heart of _____ _____ by your Holy Spirit,[18] thereby enabling _____ to always reach out to others in love. Fill him/her with your Spirit, Father.[19]

References: (1) Ephesians 4:23; (2) Psalms 18:30; (3) Proverbs 3:5-6; (4) Acts 8:21; (5) Psalms 139:23; (6) 1 John 1:9; (7) Hebrews 12:15; (8) Romans 7:6; (9) Ephesians 4:32; (10) Philippians 2:13; (11) 1 Peter 2:17, NIV; (12) 2 Peter 1:7; (13) 1 Corinthians 12:25-26; (14) Micah 6:8; (15) Isaiah 41:6; (16) Matthew 5:44; (17) Galatians 6:1; (18) Romans 5:5; (19) Ephesians 5:18.*

Being Filled With the Spirit

Key Thought: Jesus Christ says, "Be filled with the Spirit."

Key Scripture: *And be not drunk with wine, wherein is excess; but be filled* [continuously filled] *with the Spirit; Speaking to yourselves in psalms and hymns and spiritual songs, singing and making melody in your heart to the Lord; Giving thanks always for all things unto God and the Father in the name of our Lord Jesus Christ (Eph. 5:18-20).*

Prayer: Dear heavenly Father, thank you for fulfilling your promise and sending the Holy Spirit to be with us forever.[1] He is our Comforter,[2] guide,[3] helper,[4] strengthener,[5] the Spirit of truth.[3]

Thank you for your promise to give the Holy Spirit to those who ask you.[6] Thank you also for explaining that this blessed gift is a promise for my child(ren) as well.[7]

I pray that you would fill my child, _____ _____, with your Spirit continuously, and that he/she would walk in the Spirit and not fulfill the lusts of the flesh that rule so many in the world today.[8]

May he/she live in such a way that he/she would never grieve the Holy Spirit.[9] Help him/her to follow the leading of your Spirit, for as many as are led by your Spirit are your children, Lord.[10]

As _____ is filled with your Spirit, I pray that he/she would enjoy the blessing you promised of speaking to himself/herself in Psalms, hymns and spiritual songs, singing and making melody in his/her heart to you, Lord. Lead him/her to give thanks always for all things unto you, O God, our Father, in the name of our Lord Jesus Christ.[11]

I pray that _____ would so yield to your Spirit's indwelling that the fruits of love, joy, peace, patience, gentleness, goodness, faithfulness, meekness and self-control (temperance) would grow and mature in his/her life, for against such things there is no law.[12]

References: *(1) John 14:16; (2) John 15:26; (3) John 16:13; (4) Hebrews 13:6; (5) Ephesians 3:16; (6) Luke 11:13; (7) Acts 2:39; (8) Galatians 5:16; (9) Ephesians 4:30; (10) Romans 8:14; (11) Ephesians 5:18-20; (12) Galatians 5:22-23.*

The Birth of a Baby

Key Thought: A baby is a bundle of divine potential.

Key Scripture: *"For this child I prayed; and the Lord hath given me my petition which I asked of him: Therefore also I have lent him to the Lord; as long as he liveth he shall be lent to the Lord" (1 Sam. 1:27-28).*

Prayer: Heavenly Father, I come to you now with a heart filled with gratitude and adoration on the occasion of the birth of _____. Thank you for this child. I welcome him/her into our family with joy and expectancy. Bless him/her, strengthen him/her, keep him/her healthy, and guide his/her life always.

It is wonderful to realize that children are an inheritance that you bequeath to us; the fruit of the womb is a reward from you.[1] Thank you, Father, for _____ _____, and for the wonderful blessings he/she brings to us.

May _____ be filled with wisdom, Lord, thereby making my heart glad.[2] I know that the parents of a wise child shall always have joy from him/her.[3] Teach _____ that true wisdom comes from honoring you,[4] and grant him/her a heart that desires your wisdom, understanding and knowledge.[5]

As arrows are in the hand of a mighty man, so are the children of one's youth. Happy is the parent who has a full quiver of children.[6] Help me always to remember this important truth, and to always be thankful for _____ _____, even when he/she makes mistakes.

As Isaiah pointed out, a little child often leads us into the most important understanding of life.[7] Let me learn from _____, Lord, as through him/her you remind me of my need for the child-like qualities of trust, love, faith, hope, and joy. So bless the life of _____ that he/she will lead others into such wonderful knowledge.

Out of the mouths of children and infants you have ordained praise, O Lord.[8] I want to learn how to praise and trust you completely and I pray that this child will want this too.

Prevent anyone from ever abusing _____ _____. Help all family members and authority figures in his/her life always remember that whosoever shall offend one of your little ones that believe in you, it would be better for such an individual to have a millstone tied around his/her neck and to be cast into the sea rather than to hurt this precious little one.[9] Keep _____ safe at all times (10).

Teach _____ to love you, obey you and to honor his/her elders throughout his/her life.[11] In so doing, Lord, I know it will be well with him/her and his/her days will be long upon the earth.[12] Thank you, Father.

References: *(1) Psalms 127:3; (2) Proverbs 15:20; (3) Proverbs 23:24; (4) Psalms 111:10; (5) Proverbs 2:6; (6) Psalms 127:4-5; (7) Isaiah 11:6; (8) Matthew 21:16, NIV; (9) Mark 9:42; (10) Psalms 12:5; (11) Ephesians 6:1; (12) Ephesians 6:2-3.*

Caring Christian Friends

Key Thought: A true friend loves at all times.

Key Scripture: *"A man that hath friends must shew himself friendly: and there is a friend that sticketh closer than a brother" (Prov. 18:24).*

Prayer: Heavenly Father, you sent your Son, Jesus Christ, to be a propitiation for our sins.[1] I thank you that He is our abiding Friend who sticks closer than a brother.[2] Help my son/daughter to realize that you have called him/her to be a friend of Jesus,[3] and may he/she always realize that friendship with the world is hatred against you.[4]

Peer group pressure is a real threat to young people in our world today, Lord. I pray that you will so fill my child's life that he/she would always seek your approval first rather than the approval of the peer group.[5]

Bring many Christian friends to my son/daughter — friends who will love him/her at all times.[6] Help my child, _____ , to be a true friend to all those you bring to him/her.[7] May my child and his/her friends learn to bear one another's burdens in prayer and encouragement so that they will fulfill your law of love, O Lord.[8] May his/her Christian friends be the type that your Word describes, Father, friends who love at all times, remain faithful in times of adversity and who are willing, if need be, to lay down their lives for one another.[9] Help my son/daughter to be that kind of friend as well.

Your Son has declared that we are His friends if we do whatsoever He commands us to do.[10] So work in the life of my son/daughter, Lord, that he/she will always be an obedient, faithful servant who will be able to proclaim, "What a friend we have in Jesus."

References: *(1) 1 John 4:10; (2) Proverbs 18:24; (3) John 15:15; (4) James 4:4, NIV; (5) 2 Timothy 2:15; (6) Proverbs 17:17; (7) Proverbs 18:24; (8) Galatians 6:2; (9) 1 John 3:16; (10) John 15:14.*

Character and Integrity

Key Thought: Strength of character leads to courage.

Key Scripture: *"The integrity of the upright shall guide them: but the perverseness of transgressors shall destroy them" (Prov. 11:3).*

Prayer: Heavenly Father, strengthen the character of my son/daughter, _____, by enabling him/her to conquer every temptation that comes to him/her. Help _____ to ever be true to what he/she knows is right, to lean on you for the strength he/she needs,[1] so that he/she will always be able to walk in integrity of heart.[2] Let his/her Christian integrity guide him/her in every situation; may it rule in the face of every temptation.

Help my son/daughter to realize that the temptations that come to him/her are common to people everywhere. At the same time, Lord, I ask that you would help him/her to know your strength, wisdom and power in the face of temptations. Let _____ know that you will always provide him/her with a way to escape that will enable him/her to bear up in the face of all testings and trials.[3]

Always make grace abound in the life of my son/daughter, Father, and lead him/her to walk in the integrity of godly character.[4] May his/her walk ever be consistent before you, O Lord.

Fill my son/daughter with integrity of heart, and help him/her to always strive to be like Jesus who refused to abandon His integrity in the midst of difficult circumstances.[5]

Keep the soul of _____, Lord, and deliver him/her from all evil.[6] I pray that he/she would never be ashamed to have placed his/her trust in you. Let integrity and uprightness preserve him/her as he/she learns to wait on you.[7]

With your help, heavenly Father, my son/daughter will walk in integrity and uprightness of heart. Redeem him/her and be merciful unto him/her.[8] Feed him/her according to the integrity of his/her heart and guide him/her by the skillfulness of your hands.[9] Let your integrity and skill emanate from his/her life throughout his/her life.

Lead _____ to see that the issues of life spring from the heart, and as a person thinks in his heart, so is he.[10] Give _____ the grace to keep his/her heart with all diligence, Lord,[11] and the willingness always to act in accord with what his/her heart knows is right.

References: *(1) Luke 1:51; (2) Genesis 20:6; (3) 1 Corinthians 10:13; (4) 2 Corinthians 9:8; (5) Job 27:5; (6) Luke 11:4; (7) Psalms 25:21; (8) Psalms 26:11; (9) Psalms 78:72; (10) Proverbs 23:7; (11) Proverbs 4:23.*

Consecration

Key Thought: God consecrates us to do His will.

Key Scripture: *"But as he which hath called you is holy, so be ye holy in all manner of conversation; Because it is written, Be ye holy; for I am holy" (1 Pet. 1:15-16).*

Prayer: Holy Father, sanctify and consecrate my son/daughter, _____ , through your Word of truth.[1] May his/her life ever be totally consecrated unto you and your service. Show him/her the importance of coming out of the world and separating himself/herself as unto you. Keep him/her from ever touching those things that are unclean, O Lord.[2] I ask that always in the life of my child that you would lead him/her to present his/her body unto you as a living sacrifice. I know that you will find the offering of his/her life unto you to be holy and acceptable; therefore, teach _____ _____ that this is his/her spiritual act of worship.[3] Give him/her the determination not to be conformed to this world. Transform him/her, Lord, and renew his/her mind so that he/she will be able to prove what your good and acceptable and perfect will is.[4]

Show _____ that in order to ascend your hill, O Lord, he/she must be totally consecrated unto you — set apart for your service. Show him/her that his/her hands must be clean and his/her heart must be pure. Help him/her to achieve these goals, and keep him/her from ever lifting up his/her soul unto vanity. Purge him/her of all guile and deceitfulness.[5] Let the love of his/her heart, both for you and others, always be without hypocrisy, Master, I pray.[6]

You are so very holy, and the whole earth is full of your glory.[7] I pray that the life of my son/daughter will glorify you at all times, Father, because I believe that you sanctified his/her life before birth.[8] You have chosen _____ from before the foundations of the world.[9] You have called him/her to bear much fruit.[10] Thank you for your great mercy and love.

Help _____ to teach your people — both by word and deed — the important distinction that must be made between the holy and the profane.[11] Let his/her life be holiness unto you, Father.[12] Your wonderful Word will keep his/her life clean.[13] It will sanctify him/her.[14] Bless _____'s life and let it be consecrated, Lord, to thee.

May his/her prayer of consecration be like the one prayed by the Lord Jesus, "Not my will, Father, but thy will be done."[15]

References: (1) John 17:17; (2) 2 Corinthians 6:17; (3) Romans 12:1, NIV; (4) Romans 12:2; (5) Psalms 24:3-4; (6) Romans 12:9; (7) Isaiah 6:3; (8) Jeremiah 1:5; (9) Matthew 25:34; (10) John 15:16; (11) Ezekiel 44:23; (12) Zechariah 14:20; (13) John 15:3; (14) John 17:17; (15) Matthew 26:39.

Disciplining Your Child

Key Thought: The focus of discipline is on helping not punishing.

Key Scripture: *"Train up a child in the way he should go: and when he is old, he will not depart from it" (Prov. 22:6).*

Prayer: Heavenly Father, thank you for giving me the privilege of training, teaching, disciplining and leading my child, _____. Help me to remember that discipline involves the kind of training that will make one a fruitful disciple of Jesus Christ, our Lord. I join with you, Father, in helping my son/daughter to become a fruitful disciple of Jesus.

Thank you for your discipline in my life, Lord. I know that your love for me motivates you to discipline me as I need it.[1] Give me the grace to let love always be my motivation in my discipline of _____.

As you guide me with your eye, Father,[2] help me to guide my child with my eyes clearly focused on you, the Author and Finisher of our faith.[3] Thank you for teaching me your ways;[4] help me to teach your ways to my son/daughter, both by word and example.

Keep me from provoking my child to wrath, Lord.[5] Help me to bring him/her up in your nurture and admonition.[6] Set a watch before my lips, O Lord.[7] Keep me tender-hearted, full of mercy and forgiving in my relationship with my son/daughter.[8] May I always walk in your ways before him/her,[9] for I realize that your way is perfect and your Word is true.[10]

Help me not to withhold correction from my son/daughter,[11] but always to administer the appropriate discipline with firmness and with love. Give me your wisdom, Lord,[12] as I endeavor to deal with my child consistently in love.

Help me to seek my child's best interests, and to always respond to him/her with love and grace rather than reacting in anger and criticism. When he/she is overtaken in a fault, help me to restore him/her in a spirit of meekness, always cognizant of my own limitations and mistakes.[13] May I never forget the lessons you taught me as I was growing up, and help me to appreciate the special person you have created my child to be.[14]

References: (1) Hebrews 12:6; (2) Psalms 32:8; (3) Hebrews 12:2; (4) Psalms 25:4; (5) Ephesians 6:4; (6) Ephesians 6:4; (7) Psalms 141:3; (8) Ephesians 4:32; (9) Ephesians 2:10; (10) Psalms 18:30; (11) Proverbs 23:13; (12) James 1:5-6; (13) Galatians 6:1; (14) Psalms 139:14.

Enthusiasm for the Things of God

Key Thought: Enthusiasm is the result of being inspired by God.

Key Scripture: *"But seek ye first the kingdom of God, and his righteousness; and all these things shall be added unto you" (Matt. 6:33).*

Prayer: Heavenly Father, I come to you now in behalf of my son/daughter, _____. I pray that he/she will always have a hunger and a thirst for righteousness because I know you always fill the hungry heart.[1] Grant unto him/her a continual consciousness of your presence and a realization that you see him/her at all times.[2] I thank you that you are always a very present help in times of trouble.[3]

Impart to my son/daughter, O Lord, a hunger for your Word so that he/she will learn your perfect ways.[4] Help him/her to delight to do your will at all times.[5] Lead him/her to know that your joy is his/her strength.[6] May he/she always seek to put you first in his/her life.[7]

Thank you for my son/daughter, Lord. May he/she see my enthusiasm for you and thereby be moved to be filled with your Spirit who is the source of the power to witness, overcome and succeed.[8] May _____

_____ always be an enthusiastic witness for you, Lord, and heartily do all things as unto you.[9]

Give my son/daughter a spiritual hunger, Father, and help him/her to realize that those who come to your Son, Jesus Christ, will never hunger because He is the Bread of Life. Grant my son/daughter the precious gift of faith, Lord, so that he/she will always know that anyone who believes in you shall never thirst.[10] Give to my son/daughter the spirit of wisdom and revelation in the knowledge of your Son so that he/she would ever be enthused by the exceeding greatness of your power to all who believe in you.[11]

Lastly, Lord, I pray that my child will love you enthusiastically with all his/her heart, soul, mind and strength all the days of his/her life.[12]

References: *(1) Matthew 5:6; (2) Job 28:10; (3) Psalms 46:1; (4) Psalms 18:30; (5) Psalms 40:8; (6) Nehemiah 8:10; (7) Matthew 6:33; (8) Acts 1:8; (9) Colossians 3:23; (10) John 6:35; (11) Ephesians 1:17-19; (12) Mark 12:30.*

Fortitude

Key Thought: Fortitude is keeping on keeping on.

Key Scripture: *"They that wait upon the Lord shall renew their strength; they shall mount up with wings as eagles; they shall run, and not be weary" (Isa. 40:31).*

Prayer: Dear Savior and Lord, I come to you in prayer, asking you to impart fortitude to the character of my son/daughter, _____. Give him/her the grace to keep on fighting the good fight of faith throughout his/her life.[1] May he/she ever rest in the certain knowledge that you are his/her strength[2] and you will always make his/her way perfect.[3]

O God, strengthen his/her hands.[4] Always be his/her refuge and strength, a very present help to him/her in times of trouble.[5] I beseech you, Father, to help him/her to know that you are the strength of his/her heart and his/her portion forever.[6] Whenever he/she is reviled, give him/her the grace to bless those who revile him/her; whenever he/she is persecuted, give him/her the grace to endure it through fortitude.[7]

I desire, dear Lord, for my son/daughter to be strong in you at all times, ever leaning on the power of your might.[8] Keep him/her strong in the grace that is in Jesus

Christ.[9] Enable him/her to lift up his/her hands to you even in times of weariness and stress.[10]

May my son/daughter hold fast until the time of the return of Jesus Christ.[11] May he/she never grow weary in well doing as he/she realizes that he/she will reap in due season.[12] Help him/her to endure hardness as a good soldier of Jesus Christ.[13] Guide him/her to hold fast the profession of his/her faith without wavering.[14] Give him/her your hope until the end.[15] Make him/her aware that the ones who overcome will inherit all things.[16] I pray that he/she will ever stand fast in the faith.[17]

Always remind _____ , Lord, that when he/she seeks you, you will be found.[18] Let the theme of his/her life be that he/she would do everything heartily as unto you, O Lord, and not unto men.[19]

References: *(1) 1 Timothy 6:12; (2) Habakkuk 3:19; (3) 2 Samuel 22:33; (4) Nehemiah 6:9; (5) Psalms 46:1; (6) Psalms 73:26; (7) 1 Corinthians 4:12; (8) Ephesians 6:10; (9) 2 Timothy 2:1; (10) Hebrews 12:12; (11) Revelation 2:25; (12) Galatians 6:9; (13) 2 Timothy 2:3; (14) Hebrews 10:23; (15) 1 Peter 1:13; (16) Revelation 21:7; (17) Hebrews 6:11; (18) Deuteronomy 4:29; (19) Colossians 3:23.*

Freedom From Condemnation

Key Thought: When Jesus comes, all condemnation leaves.

Key Scripture: *"For God sent not his Son into the world to condemn the world; but that the world through him might be saved. He that believeth on him is not condemned: but he that believeth not is condemned already, because he hath not believed in the name of the only begotten Son of God" (John 3:17-18).*

Prayer: Dear Lord, thank you for the wonderful freedom you have provided for your people in every area of life. Those you make free are free indeed.[1] I pray for my son/daughter, _____ , that he/she would refuse to receive condemnation in his/her life in any form, for condemnation does not come from you.[2]

When he/she does wrong, help him/her to respond to the conviction of your Spirit by confessing his/her sins to you, realizing that you will forgive him/her and you will cleanse him/her from all unrighteousness.[3] After confessing his/her sins, I pray that you will lead him/her always to walk in freedom, never again becoming entangled with any yoke of bondage.[4] Those you make free are free indeed, Lord;[5] keep _____ constantly aware of this truth and the realization that the truth will make him/her free from condemnation and every other problem.[6]

Father, reveal to _____ that the blood of Jesus Christ, your Son, cleanses him/her of all unrighteousness.[7] That through faith in your Son and in your Word, he/she is able to walk in newness of life,[8] never having to struggle with condemnation in any form. Help him/her to always want to seek to walk after your Spirit, for this is the key to knowing that your Spirit of life in Christ Jesus sets us free from the law of sin and death.[9]

In the name of Jesus Christ, my Lord and Savior, I come against the enemy of the soul of my son/daughter. Through the power of your Spirit, Lord, I reject the condemning lies and accusations that Satan, the father of lies, tries to perpetrate against my son/daughter.[10] Rebuke him, for he is the accuser of the brethren, Father,[11] the one who seeks to devour the faith the joy of my son/daughter.[12]

Always keep _____ secure in your refuge,[13] and help him/her to resist the devil by faith, fully realizing that when he/she does this, the devil, and all his lies of condemnation, will flee from him/her.[14]

Thank you for the rich and precious promises of your Word, Father.[15] I rejoice in the realization that _____ _____ (and myself) will not come into condemnation any longer, because we have passed from death to life.[16] Praise you, Lord.

References: *(1) John 8:36; (2) Romans 8:1; (3) 1 John 1:9; (4) Galatians 5:1; (5) John 8:36; (6) John 8:32; (7) 1 John 1:7; (8) Romans 6:4; (9) Romans 8:1-2; (10) John 8:44; (11) Revelation 12:10; (12) 1 Peter 5:8; (13) Psalms 91:2; (14) James 4:7; (15) 2 Peter 1:4; (16) John 5:24.*

Freedom From Fear

Key Thought: A faith-filled heart has no room for fear.

Key Scripture: *"Behold, God is my salvation; I will trust, and not be afraid: for the Lord Jehovah is my strength and my song; he also is become my salvation. Therefore with joy shall ye draw water out of the wells of salvation. And in that day shall ye say, Praise the Lord"* *(Isa. 12:2-4).*

Prayer: Lord God, I thank you that you are the light and the salvation of my son/daughter. Reveal this to him/her so that he/she will realize that you are the strength of his/her life and because this is true, he/she will not need to fear.[1] Keep my child from sudden fear, Lord, be his/her confidence, and keep his/her foot from being taken.[2]

Give my son/daughter, _____, your peace and keep his/her heart from ever being afraid, Lord. Thank you for your gift of peace that is available to each of us through your Son.[3]

Show _____ that he/she has not received the spirit of bondage again to fear but he/she has received the Spirit of adoption that makes him/her cry, "Abba, Father." May this be the cry of my son/daughter at all times, Lord, as he/she realizes all that it means to be adopted into your family.[4]

Realizing the truth of your Word, Lord, that you will never leave him/her nor forsake him/her, may he/she boldly say, "The Lord is my helper, I will not fear what man shall do unto me.[5]

There is no fear in your love, Father. Your perfect loves casts out all fear.[6] Deliver my son/daughter from all the torments of fear. Fill him/her with your love as he/she receives it by faith in your promise that your love is shed abroad in his/her heart by the Holy Spirit.[7]

Teach _____ to seek you with all his/her heart. Let him/her know that you hear him/her and you will always deliver him/her from all fear.[8] May your loving presence assure him/her that you are with him/her, giving him/her peace and wiping away all his/her fears.[9] Give him/her the grace to refuse all fear as he/she stands still and waits for your salvation.[10] You, Lord, will fight for him/her and you will give him/her peace. Empower him/her with your Spirit so that he/she will neither fear nor be discouraged because he/she will know that you are with him/her and you have not given him/her a spirit of fear, but of power and of love and of a sound mind.[11]

Thank you, Lord, for being _____ _____'s refuge and his/her strength, a very present help to him/her in times of trouble and chaos. Show this truth to him/her so that he/she will never fear, even though the earth be removed and the mountains be carried into the sea.[12] Help him/her to determine to fear no evil in light of the fact that you are with him/her and your rod and staff bring comfort to him/her.[13]

References: *(1) Psalms 27:1; (2) Proverbs 3:25-26; (3) John 14:27; (4) Romans 8:15-16; (5) Hebrews 13:6; (6) 1 John 4:18; (7) Romans 5:5; (8) Psalms 34:4; (9) Genesis 26:24; (10) Exodus 14:13; (11) 2 Timothy 1:7; (12) Psalms 46:1-2; (13) Psalms 23:4.*

Freedom From Guilt

Key Thought: God always forgives the repentant heart.

Key Scripture: *"If we confess our sins, he is faithful and just to forgive us our sins, and to cleanse us from all unrighteousness" (1 John 1:9).*

Prayer: Lord God, I thank you for the grace of forgiveness that you so freely share with your children. Show my son/daughter, _____, that he/she has an advocate with you who is Jesus Christ, your Son. I thank you that Jesus is the propitiation for our sins, and I ask you to remind _____ of this truth whenever guilt from sin enters his/her conscience.[1] Always grant repentance to his/her heart, I pray, so that he/she will always want to turn away from his/her sins and determine to follow you.[2]

Reveal to _____ that by taking heed according to your Word, he/she will be able to keep his/her way clean and pure.[3] I ask, Father, that you will draw him/her so strongly to you that he/she will always want to seek you with his/her whole heart. Don't ever let him/her wander from your commandments, Father. May he/she hide your Word in his/her heart so that he/she will not sin against you.[4]

Show _____ that guilt no longer has dominion in his/her life. You have set him/her free from all guilt and condemnation through the sacrifice of your Son which has cleansed him/her from all sin. I thank you for justifying my son/daughter, for seeing him/her as if he/she has never sinned and I pray that he/she will be able to look upon his/her life the same way, Father. Impute your righteousness to him/her. How I praise you that your Son, who knew no sin, became sin for us so that righteousness would be revealed in us who believe.[5] Let this process take place in the life of my child.

Unto you, O Lord, I lift up my soul, for you are good and you are always ready to forgive. You are plenteous in mercy unto all who call upon you.[6] Lead _____ _____ to call upon you with the confidence that comes from knowing that you hear us and you will provide mercy to help in his/her time of need.[7]

Lead _____ to covenant with you, Father, to put away all bitterness, wrath, anger, clamor and evil speaking, along with all malice. Give him/her the heart's desire to always endeavor to be kind to others, tender-hearted and compassionate and always forgiving, even as you for Christ's sake have forgiven him/her.[8]

References: *(1) 1 John 2:1-2; (2) Acts 11:18; (3) Psalms 119:9; (4) Psalms 119:11; (5) 2 Corinthians 5:21; (6) Psalms 86:4-6; (7) Hebrews 4:16; (8) Ephesians 4:30-32.*

Freedom From Selfishness

Key Thought: The middle letter in the word "sin" is I.

Key Scripture: *"Whosoever shall seek to save his life shall lose it; and whosoever shall lose his life shall preserve it" (Luke 17:33).*

Prayer: Our loving Lord, I thank you for my son/daughter, _____. I pray that you will keep him/her from all selfishness as he/she realizes that his/her life is not his/her own, but it was bought by the price of the blood your Son shed for us.[1] Help him/her not to think more highly of himself/herself than he/she ought to think, but to think with sober judgment, according to the measure of faith you have imparted to him/her.[2]

I pray that _____ will always be a tender-hearted and forgiving person.[3] Keep him/her from the sin of pride that always goes before a fall.[4] Teach him/her to find his/her rightful place under your Lordship.[5]

Reveal to my son/daughter that everyone who loves his/her life shall lose it, but he/she that hates his/her life in this world shall keep it unto life eternal.[6] Burn into the heart of my son/daughter the truth that you have revealed in your Word: "Whoso stoppeth his ears at the cry of the poor, he also shall cry himself, but shall not be heard."[7]

Lead _____ to see that of himself or herself nothing can be accomplished. Keep him/her from seeking his/her own will instead of yours.[8] Motivate him/her to seek you and your righteousness first at all times,[9] and help him/her to lay up treasures for himself/herself in heaven where nothing can decay or corrupt them.[10]

Give him/her the empathy it requires to bear the burdens of others so that he/she will be able to fulfill your law, O Lord.[11] May he/she never grow weary in well-doing;[12] lead him/her to be a generous person at all times. I pray that _____ will always strive to be blameless (as your steward); keep him/her from ever being self-willed, angry, greedy or corrupt in any way.   Instead, I pray that he/she will always be hospitable, a lover of good, self-controlled, upright, holy and disciplined.   I ask you, Father, to empower _____ to hold fast the faithful Word as he/she has been taught, that he/she may be able by sound doctrine both to encourage others and refute those who oppose it.[13]

References: (1) 1 Corinthians 6:19-20; (2) Romans 12:3; (3) Ephesians 4:32; (4) Proverbs 16:18 ; (5) 2 Timothy 1:2; (6) John 12:25; (7) Proverbs 21:13; (8) John 5:30; (9) Matthew 6:33; (10) Matthew 6:20; (11) Galatians 6:2; (12) Galatians 6:9; (13) Titus 1:7-9, NIV.*

Freedom From Worldliness

Key Thought: A double-minded person is unstable in every way.

Key Scripture: *"I beseech you therefore, brethren, by the mercies of God, that ye present your bodies a living sacrifice, holy, acceptable unto God, which is your reasonable service. And be not conformed to this world: but be ye transformed by the renewing of your mind, that ye may prove what is that good, and acceptable, and perfect, will of God" (Rom. 12:1-2).*

Prayer: O God, our loving Father, I love you. Thank you for my son/daughter, _____. I pray for him/her, asking you to keep him/her focused on the things that are important to you rather than the things that are important to this world.

I pray that he/she will never be conformed to this world, but will always seek to be transformed by the renewing of his/her mind so that he/she will be able to know and follow your will.[1]

Help him/her to realize that friendship with the world is enmity against you,[2] that he/she is a citizen of a different kingdom than that which is represented by this world and that he/she needs to deny all worldly lusts and ungodliness in order to live soberly, righteously and godly in this present world.[3]

Show my son/daughter that you have made the wisdom of this world foolish,[4] that the god of this world has blinded the minds of many[5] and the sorrow of this world works death.[6]

I pray that _____ will always be an ambassador of your Kingdom, Father.[7] May he/she always shine as a light in this world.[8] Keep him/her unspotted from this world, Lord.[9]

Help _____ to know that the fashions of this world pass away,[10] but your Word will never pass away.[11] Let no one beguile him/her of his/her reward in a voluntary humility and the worshiping of angels.[12] Prevent him/her from ever walking according to the course of this world, according to the prince of the power of the air, the spirit that now works in the children of disobedience.[13] Deliver _____ from this present evil world, according to your will, O Father.[14]

I pray that my son/daughter will not love the world or the things of this world. Instead, Lord, I ask that he/she would learn to love you at all times — with all his/her heart, soul, mind and strength[15] — fully realizing that if someone loves the world, your love is not in that person.[16] Strengthen him/her by your Holy Spirit to resist the pulls of this world, Father — the pride of life, the lust of the eyes and the lust of the flesh.[17]

References: (1) Romans 12:1-2; (2) James 4:4; (3) Titus 2:12; (4) 1 Corinthians 1:20; (5) 2 Corinthians 4:4; (6) 2 Corinthians

7:10; (7) 2 Corinthians 5:20; (8) Philippians 2:15; (9) James 1:27; (10) 1 Corinthians 7:31; (11) Matthew 24:35; (12) Colossians 2:18; (13) Ephesians 2:2; (14) Galatians 1:4; (15) Matthew 22:37; (16) 1 John 2:15; (17) 1 John 2:16.

Freedom From Worry

Key Thought: Trust in God.

Key Scripture: *"And we know that all things work together for good to them that love God, to them who are the called according to his purpose" (Rom. 8:28).*

Prayer: Thank you, Father, for giving your children freedom from worry, anxiety and fear. I pray for my son/daughter, Lord, that you would teach him/her to cast all his/her cares upon you in the full realization that you care for him/her.[1] Let him/her know that your constant invitation is to come unto you in order to find rest and freedom from worry.[2]

Show _____ that in the light of eternity few things are worthy of concern, because nothing shall be able to separate him/her from your love in Christ Jesus our Lord — not things past or present, nor things yet to come.[3] Reassure him/her that you are continually working your purposes out in his/her life and that you are the Master of all circumstances. I pray that he/she will learn how to trust you early in life, believing, Lord, that you will supply all his/her needs according to your riches in glory.[4]

Lead him/her out of all fear, anxiety and worry through your everlasting love for him/her. I pray that

_____ will always know that your perfect love casts out all fear.[5] You have told us, Father, not to fear because it is your good pleasure to give us your Kingdom.[6] Speak this truth to the heart of my son/daughter.

Lord, help him/her to obey your command not to worry about anything. I pray that he/she will be anxious for nothing, but will learn to spend his/her time in your Word and in prayer and supplication, letting his/her requests be made known unto you with thanksgiving. As he/she learns to do this, I pray that your peace which surpasses all understanding will guard his/her heart and mind through Christ Jesus.[7] Lord, I am so very thankful that you have provided prayer and praise as practical outlets to prevent us from worrying.

Give _____ the grace not to worry about tomorrow, realizing that tomorrow will take care of itself. Let him/her learn to take one day at a time, Lord, because you have shown us that this day's trouble is enough for one day.[8]

Lead my son/daughter to stand on the promises of your Word, Father, for your Word is the perfect antidote for worry in that it builds faith in our hearts.[9] Thank you for taking good care of _____. I place his/her hand in yours, knowing that you always take good care of your children.[10]

References: (1) 1 Peter 5:7; (2) Matthew 11:28; (3) Romans 8:38-39; (4) Philippians 4:19; (5) 1 John 4:18; (6) Luke 12:32; (7) Philippians 4:6-7, NKJV; (8) Matthew 6:34; (9) Romans 10:17; (10) 2 Timothy 1:12.

Godliness and Holiness

Key Thought: "To be holy and not happy is a contradiction" (Anonymous).

Key Scripture: *"Give unto the Lord, O ye mighty, give unto the Lord glory and strength. Give unto the Lord the glory due unto his name; worship the Lord in the beauty of holiness" (Ps. 29:1-2).*

Prayer: Teach my son/daughter, O Lord, the beauty of holiness.[1] Show him/her the importance of giving you the glory that is due unto your name, and to worship you in the beauty of holiness.[2] May he/she never trade the beauty of holiness for anything, no matter how attractive or appealing it may be. Lord, I beseech you to lead him/her into the happiness that comes from being pure in heart, so that he/she will be able to see you.[3]

Grant, Almighty God, that my son/daughter would always be delivered out of the hand of his/her enemies so that he/she would learn to serve you without fear in holiness and righteousness all the days of his/her life.[4] Reveal to _____ that you divine power has given him/her everything he/she needs for life and godliness.[5] So work in his/her heart, Father, that he/she will earnestly desire to pursue righteousness, godliness, faith, love, endurance and gentleness.[6]

Give my son/daughter an earnest desire to perfect your holiness out of respect and reverence for you and your name.[7] May he/she ever strive to be renewed in the spirit of his/her mind so that he/she would always be able to put on the new man which is created in righteousness and true holiness. Lead him/her to put away all lying and to speak truth at all times.[8]

Establish the heart of my son/daughter in unblameable holiness before you, O Lord, so that when Jesus Christ comes again, he/she will be able to stand before Him without shame.[9] I pray that my son/daughter will always strive to follow peace with all people and to live a holy life before you.[10] Let him/her understand even now that godliness with contentment is great gain.[11]

References: (1) 1 Chronicles 16:29; (2) Psalms 29:2; (3) Matthew 5:8; (4) Luke 1:75; (5) 2 Peter 1:3, NIV; (6) 1 Timothy 6:11; (7) 2 Corinthians 7:1; (8) Ephesians 4:24-25; (9) 1 Thessalonians 3:13; (10) Hebrews 12:14; (11) 1 Timothy 6:6.

The Grieving Child

Key Thought: All comfort comes from God.

Key Scripture: *"The Lord is nigh unto them that are of a broken heart; and saveth such as be of a contrite spirit" (Ps. 34:18).*

Prayer: Loving heavenly Father, the God of all comfort,[1] I ask you to be a very present help[2] to my son/daughter, _____, as he/she faces the loss of _____. Draw him/her to pour out his/her heart before you, and I pray that as he/she does so, he/she will clearly recognize that you are his/her refuge.[3]

Thank you for being the Good Shepherd to _____ _____,[4] for leading him/her beside the still waters and for restoring his/her soul. Make him/her to lie down in green pastures, and lead him/her in the paths of righteousness for your name's sake. Reassure his/her heart that he/she need not fear any evil because you are with him/her, and your rod and staff bring comfort to him/her.[5] Thank you for giving comfort to my child, Lord.

Show _____ that all who mourn will be comforted.[6] Let him/her know that you will indeed turn his/her mourning into dancing,[7] that you always heal the broken in heart,[8] and that you will bind up his/her wounds.[9] Turn his/her sorrow into joy, O Lord,[10] and remind my son/daughter that you have overcome the world and its sorrows.[11] Reveal to _____ _____ that the time will come when there will be no more death, sorrow, crying, and pain.[12]

Impart to his/her heart your peace which surpasses all understanding.[13] Give him/her a quiet assurance that even though weeping may endure for a night, joy will come in the morning.[14] Help me to weep with him/her,[15] and to give him/her the same comfort that you have given to me during times of loss.[16]

Increase his/her faith in you[17] as he/she goes through this time. Restore to him/her the joy of your salvation.[18] I pray that he/she will be able to reach out and take your hand by faith, trusting in you with all his/her heart and leaning not unto his/her own understanding. Even during this time of grief, Father, I pray that he/she will find the grace to acknowledge you and to realize that you will direct his/her paths.[19] Thank you for blessing _____ _____'s life with healing,[20] hope,[21] love,[22] faith,[23] confidence,[24] and peace.[25] As he/she draws near to you, I ask you to draw near to him/her.[26] Thank you , Lord.

References: *(1) 2 Corinthians 1:3; (2) Psalms 46:1; (3) Psalms 62:8; (4) John 10:11; (5) Psalms 23; (6) Matthew 5:4; (7) Psalms 30:11; (8) Luke 4:18; (9) Psalms 147:3; (10) John 16:20; (11) John 16:33; (12) Revelation 21:4; (13) Philippians 4:7; (14) Psalms 30:5; (15) Romans 12:15; (16) 2 Corinthians 1:4; (17) Luke 17:5; (18) Psalms 51:12; (19) Proverbs 3:5-6; (20) Isaiah 61:1; (21) Colossians 1:23; (22) Romans 8:28; (23) 1 Corinthians 16:13; (24) 2 Thessalonians 2:2; (25) John 14:27; (26) James 4:8.*

Growing in Christ

Key Thought: God's Word produces spiritual growth.

Key Scripture: *"But speaking the truth in love, may grow up into him in all things, which is the head, even Christ" (Eph. 4:15).*

Prayer: Thank you, Lord, that spiritual growth is a normal part of the Christian life, and that you are helping my child _____ to grow in the Lord Jesus. You are at work in him/her, Father, both to will and to do your good pleasure.[1] Thank you for nurturing him/her and leading him/her each step of the way.

Help my child to lay aside all malice, and all guile, and hypocrisies, and envies, and all evil speakings; and as a newborn baby to desire the sincere milk of the word that he/she may grow thereby.[2]

Let _____, as a lively, living stone, be built up as a member of your spiritual house, a royal priesthood, to offer up spiritual sacrifices acceptable to you, O God, by Jesus Christ.[3]

May he/she fulfill your Word by speaking the truth in love, and thereby grow up into Christ in all things, because He is the Head.[4]

Thank you for helping _____,
Father, to grow in grace, and in the knowledge of the
Lord Jesus Christ. To Him be glory both now and
forever. Amen.[5]

References: (1) Philippians 2:13; (2) 1 Peter 2:1-2; (3) 1 Peter
2:5; (4) Ephesians 4:15; (5) 2 Peter 3:18.

Happiness

Key Thought: "Happiness is...the union of ourselves with God" (Blaise Pascal).

Key Scripture: *"Correct thy son, and he shall give thee rest; yea, he shall give delight unto thy soul. Where there is no vision, the people perish: but he that keepeth the law, happy is he" (Prov. 29:17-18).*

Prayer: Father of lights, with whom there is no variableness or shadow of turning,[1] I beseech you to grant happiness to my son/daughter throughout this life and the life to come. Help him/her to understand your truth that happiness comes from obeying you.[2] When it becomes necessary for you to correct him/her, help him/her to be happy in the certain knowledge that you are at work in his/her life; may he/she never despise your chastening, Lord.[3]

I thank you, Father, that the hope of the righteous is gladness.[4] Keep the heart of my son/daughter happy and glad before you because I know that a merry heart will be like a medicine to him/her.[5] Reveal the keys to happiness that your Son showed us in the Sermon on the Mount: peace, meekness, humility, spiritual hunger, mercy and purity.[6] Help him/her to seek these qualities at all times in his/her life.

Keep the heart of my son/daughter merry, Lord, and may he/she always show his/her glad-heartedness with a cheerful countenance.[7] Put gladness in his/her heart, O Lord,[8] and anoint him/her with the oil of joy as he/she learns to love righteousness and hate wickedness.[9] I thank you, Father, that the hope of the righteous is found in the gladness you impart to the human heart.[10]

Remind _____ regularly, Lord, that in your presence is fullness of joy and at your right hand are pleasures forevermore.[11] Reveal to him/her that you inhabit the praises of your people[12] and that you rejoice over him/her with singing.[13] Help him/her to speak to himself/herself in psalms and hymns and spiritual songs, making melody in his/her heart unto you, Lord, giving thanks always for all things unto you, Father, in Jesus name.[14]

Fill the heart of my son/daughter with gladness, Lord, and give him/her the wisdom to see that true gladness and happiness come from following you.[15]

References: (1) James 1:17; (2) Proverbs 29:18; (3) Job 5:17; (4) Proverbs 10:28; (5) Proverbs 17:22; (6) Matthew 5:2-9; (7) Proverbs 15:13; (8) Psalms 4:7; (9) Psalms 45:7; (10) Proverbs 10:28; (11) Psalms 16:11; (12) Psalms 22:3; (13) Zephaniah 3:17; (14) Ephesians 5:19-20; (15) Acts 14:17.

Healing for Emotional Hurts

Key Thought: God applies the Balm of Gilead to every wound.

Key Scripture: *"The Spirit of the Lord is upon me, because he hath anointed me to preach the gospel to the poor; he hath sent me to heal the brokenhearted, to preach deliverance to the captives, and recovering of sight to the blind, to set at liberty them that are bruised" (Luke 4:18).*

Prayer: Lord God, I come to you now, in the name of Jesus,[1] to lift up to your loving presence my son/daughter, _____ who suffers from inner hurts due to certain experiences in his/her life. Please, dear Father, heal and cancel all the negative effects in his/her life that have resulted from: _____ _____.

As _____ learns to walk with you, I pray that you will teach him/her to trust you with all his/her heart, to lean not unto his/her own understanding. May he/she always commit his/her way unto you, constantly acknowledging your healing presence in his/her life, and I know you will direct his/her paths.[2]

Teach him/her your ways.[3] I pray that he/she will hide your Word in his/her heart so that he/she will not sin againt you.[4] Reveal to _____ that a young person (as well as all other people) will be able to cleanse his/her way by taking heed to your Word.⁵

Help _____ to stand fast in the liberty wherewith Christ has made him/her free. I pray that he/she would never again be entangled with any yoke of bondage.⁶ Help him/her to forgive any who may have have wronged him/her,⁷ and, Lord, I ask you to fill the gap between the love he/she should have received and the love he/she actually did receive.⁸

Reveal your love to him/her.⁹ May he/she ever walk securely in your love.¹⁰ The death of Jesus Christ on Calvary makes it wonderfully possible for _____ _____ to walk in newness of life.¹¹ This is my prayer for him/her, Lord.¹² Thank you for setting at liberty all who have been bruised;¹³ thank you for giving my son/daughter your Spirit to cheer and guide him/her,¹⁴ to bring liberty to him/her,¹⁵ and to comfort him/her.¹⁶

Dear Lord, our Good Shepherd, heal _____ _____ of all emotional hurts and scars. Lead him/her in the paths of righteousness for your name's sake.¹⁷

References: (1) John 16:24; (2) Proverbs 3:5-6; (3) Psalms 27:11; (4) Psalms 119:11; (5) Psalms 119:9; (6) Galatians 5:1; (7) Ephesians 4:32; (8) 1 John 4:18-19; (9) Romans 8:39; (10) Ephesians 3:18-20; (11) Romans 6:4; (12) Revelation 21:5; (13) Luke 4:18; (14) Psalms 48:14; (15) Romans 8:21; (16) Psalms 86:17; (17) Psalms 23:3.

Healing for Physical Illness

Key Thought: God heals because God loves.

Key Scripture: *"For I am the Lord that healeth thee"* *(Exod. 15:26).*

Prayer: Heavenly Father, thank you for your love and for your desire to heal your people. I come to you now on behalf of my child, _____ , who suffers from _____. I ask you, Lord, to heal his/her body and to restore him/her to complete health in you.

You are the Balm in Gilead,[1] Lord, and you are the one who brings healing to the human body. You created our bodies,[2] and you know exactly what we need in order to be well. Lord, you healed all who were brought to you.[3] Your Word says that you are the Lord who heals us.[4] You, Lord, take our infirmities and carry our diseases.[5] You are the same yesterday, today and forever.[6]

You tell us in your Word, Lord, to pray for one another so that we may be healed,[7] and that the prayer of faith will save the sick, and you will raise them up.[8]

In faith in your character and your Word, Lord, I now bring _____ to you, and I beseech you to heal him/her even as you healed the lame, blind and afflicted when you walked the earth.[9] All power in heaven and earth is yours, Lord.[10]   Impart your supernatural healing power to _____.

Send healing on the wings of your Spirit, Lord,[11] to him/her. You have mercifully promised to be his/her healer, so I ask you to not permit this affliction to remain with him/her.

With all that is in me, I bless your holy name and I will not forget the benefits of your great mercy, Lord. You forgive all our iniquities and you heal all our diseases.[12]

I hope in you, O Lord. I will ever praise you.[13] Thank you for being health to _____ and for healing him/her. Glory, praise and honor be to your name forever and ever.

References: *(1) Jeremiah 8:22; (2) Psalms 139:14; (3) Matthew 9:35; (4) Exodus 15:26; (5) Matthew 8:17; (6) Hebrews 13:8; (7) James 5:16; (8) James 5:15; (9) Luke 4:40; (10) Matthew 28:18; (11) Malachi 4:2; (12) Psalms 103:3; (13) Psalms 42:11.*

Other Scriptures: *Matthew 10:8, Isaiah 53:5, Psalms 107:20, Isaiah 58:8, Jeremiah 30:17, Mark 16:18, 1 Corinthians 12:28, James 5:14, 1 Peter 2:24.*

A Healthy Self-Concept

Key Thought: Each person is made in the image of God.

Key Scripture: *"I praise you because I am fearfully and wonderfully made; your works are wonderful, I know that full well. My frame was not hidden from you when I was made in the secret place. When I was woven together in the depths of the earth, your eyes saw my unformed body. All the days ordained for me were written in your book before one of them came to be" (Ps. 139:14-16, NIV).*

Prayer: Heavenly Father, I thank you for your love which is from everlasting to everlasting. Keep my son/daughter, _____, constantly aware of your amazing love and grace. Reveal to him/her that there is no condemnation to those who walk after your Spirit rather than after the flesh.[1] Show him/her how to walk after your Spirit at all times and help him/her to experience the true life and peace that are the fruits of spiritual-mindedness.[2] Help him/her to realize that nothing will be able to separate him/her from your great love,[3] except his/her own refusal to accept it.

I pray that _____ will always grow in your grace and knowledge,[4] to the extent that he/she will be able to see himself/herself as you see him/her — loved, accepted and complete in Christ Jesus.[5] I thank you that you have created him/her in your image,[6] and that Jesus died for him/her in order to set him/her free from all negative powers.

Show _____ that he/she is a new creation in Christ Jesus. Help him/her to appropriate the truth that you are transforming him/her into a wonderful, new masterpiece. The old things are gone and you are making all things new to and for him/her.[7] Thank you, Father.

Thank you for delivering him/her from the powers of darkness and translating him/her into your Kingdom.[8] Help him/her to put off the old man (including a negative self-concept) and to put on the new man which is renewed in knowledge after your image, Lord.[9] Thank you for changing _____ into your very own image, from glory to glory, by your Spirit,[10] and for enabling him/her to love himself/herself as you love him/her.

Give _____ a desire to stand spiritually mature and complete in all your will, Father.[11] Show him/her that your strength is always made perfect in our weakness, especially as he/she learns to lean on you.[12] It is so good to know that we don't have to make ourselves perfect, Father, but you are constantly molding and shaping us according to your desires. Impart this truth to my son/daughter.

References: (1) Romans 8:1; (2) Romans 8:6; (3) Romans 8:38-39; (4) 2 Peter 3:18; (5) Colossians 2:10; (6) Genesis 1:26; (7) 2 Corinthians 5:17; (8) Colossians 1:13; (9) Colossians 3:10; (10) 2 Corinthians 3:18; (11) Colossians 4:12; (12) 2 Corinthians 12:9.

The Immediate Family

Key Thought: "A happy family is but an earlier heaven" (Sir John Bowring).

Key Scripture: *"And if it seem evil unto you to serve the Lord, choose you this day whom ye will serve; whether the gods which your fathers served that were on the other side of the flood, or the gods of the Amorites, in whose land ye dwell: but as for me and my house, we will serve the Lord"* *(Josh. 24:15).*

Prayer: Heavenly Father, you are the one who sets the solitary into families,[1] and you have promised to be a Father to the fatherless.[2] I pray for our family, Lord, that you would ever watch over our comings and goings and that underneath would always be your everlasting arms.[3]

Bless our family, Lord, and keep us safe from all harm.[4] Plant your hedge of protection around us,[5] and let us dwell in safety.[6] Thank you for blessing our family with all spiritual blessings in heavenly places in Christ.[7]

Help me to remember that our home will be built through wisdom, and by understanding it will be established.[8] By knowledge shall all the chambers of our home be filled with precious and pleasant riches.[9]

Your Word, O Lord, declares that the home of the righteous shall be filled with much treasure.[10] In times of wickedness, you have promised that the house of the righteous will stand.[11] Thank you, Father. I believe this promise and I appropriate it for my home and family.

Because I believe on your Son, the Lord and Savior Jesus Christ, I know that you have saved me and I claim your promise that you will save my household.[12] Thank you, Father, for all your abundant blessings in the lives of my family members.

Teach us to pray together as a family under your Lordship. May we never forsake you. We choose to put you first, as Joshua and his household did, and we are determined to serve you all our days. Bless my spouse and my children and our extended family. Help me to put you first and to always remember to take good care of all you've given me, especially those you have placed under my care.

References: (1) Psalms 68:6; (2) Psalms 68:5; (3) Deuteronomy 33:27; (4) Proverbs 29:25; (5) Job 1:10; (6) Leviticus 25:18; (7) Ephesians 1:3; (8) Proverbs 24:3-4; (9) Proverbs 24:3-4; (10) Proverbs 15:6; (11) Proverbs 12:7; (12) Acts 16:31.

The Joy of the Lord

Key Thought: True joy comes from within; it is not based on circumstances.

Key Scripture: *"That the trial of your faith, being much more precious than gold that perisheth, though it be tried with fire, might be found unto praise and honour and glory at the appearing of Jesus Christ: Whom having not seen, ye love; in whom, though now ye see him not, yet believing, ye rejoice with joy unspeakable and full of glory" (1 Pet. 1:7-8).*

Prayer: Thank you for joy, Father. Your joy, as Nehemiah pointed out, truly is our source of strength.[1] Give joy to my son/daughter, _____, show him/her how to rejoice always, to pray without ceasing and to be thankful in everything.[2] I rejoice in you, Lord, for the child(ren) you have given to me. I will rejoice forever in all the blessings you have showered upon my family.[3]

It thrills me to know that you, the Lord God omnipotent, reign forever.[4] Impart this same sense of wonder, adoration and joy to _____ , O Lord, so that he/she will choose to magnify and exalt you, to enter through your gates with thanksgiving and to go into your courts with praise.[5] Teach him/her the power of praise and worship and show him/her that such adoration always brings joy to the human heart.

Give my son/daughter the precious gift of thankfulness — a quality too often forgotten in this present age.
Lead him/her to express his/her thanks to you often,
Father, and to believe that you are continually working
your purposes out in his/her life. So fill him/her with your
Spirit[6] that he/she will want to make a joyful noise unto
you and to serve your with gladness. Draw him/her to
your throne, Father, and as he/she obeys you with gladness, I pray that he/she will come before your presence
with singing. Let him/her express thankfulness to you,
Lord, for all that you have done and for who you are. May
he/she ever be thankful that he/she knows you as his/her
personal Lord and Savior, realizing that it is you who
made him/her and he/she is your child forever. Praise
your mighty name![7]

Give my son/daughter the constant hope, Father, that
when your glory is revealed in all its fullness, he/she will
be able to experience your exceeding great joy.[8] Reveal
the truth to him/her so that he/she will see that your mercy
is everlasting and your truth endures to all generations.[9]

Keep his/her heart merry at all times so that he/she
can experience health, vitality and joy,[10] and may he/she
draw water from the wells of your salvation[11] as the fruit
of joy grows in his/her life.[12]

References: (1) Nehemiah 8:10; (2) 1 Thessalonians 5:16-18;
(3) Philippians 4:4; (4) Revelation 19:6; (5) Psalms 100:4;
(6) Ephesians 5:18; (7) Psalms 100; (8) 1 Peter 4:13;
(9) Psalms 117:2; (10) Proverbs 17:22; (11) Isaiah 12:3;
(12) Galatians 5:22.

Knowing God

Key Thought: Christianity is not a religion; it's a relationship.

Key Scripture: *"That I may know him, and the power of his resurrection, and the fellowship of his sufferings, being made conformable unto his death"* *(Phil. 3:10).*

Prayer: Heavenly Father, I pray that my son/daughter, _____, will ever seek to know you. Teach him/her to learn how to be still and to know you as the God who is always there.[1] Thank you for choosing _____ to be your friend.[2] Betroth him/her in faithfulness, Lord, so that he/she can know you in an intimately personal way.[3]

You have promised that the people who know you will be strong and do exploits in your name and through your mighty power.[4] I pray that _____ will be such a person because he/she knows you.

Help me to be faithful to you so that I can teach my son/daughter your ways both through words and example, Lord. I desire to delight to do your will as a parent,[5] and I pray that _____ will always want to keep your commandments so that he/she will get to know you intimately.[6]

Fill _____ with the knowledge of your will in all wisdom and spiritual understanding,

Father, that he/she might walk worthy of you unto all pleasing, being fruitful in every good work, and increasing in the knowledge of you at all times.[7] I pray that he/she will always walk in the full knowledge of your Word, your will and your ways.

Strengthen him/her with all might according to your glorious power, unto all patience and longsuffering with joyfulness.[8] I give thanks to you, Father, for making _____ able to become a partaker of the inheritance of the saints of light.[9] Thank you for delivering him/her from the power of darkness and for translating him/her into the Kingdom of Jesus Christ.[10] Thank you, Father, for giving _____ redemption through the blood of your Son, along with full forgiveness of sins. May he/she fully experience the love of Christ Jesus who is the image of your eternal glory — the firstborn of every creature.[11] Jesus is before all things, and by Him all things consist.[12] Reveal this to my son/daughter, Father, so that he/she will be able to know you and to experience the abundant life you offer so freely.[13]

I pray that he/she will continually experience fellowship with you, Father, and with your Son, Jesus Christ.[14] May the grace of the Lord Jesus Christ and the love of God and the communion (fellowship) of the Holy Spirit always be with him/her.[15] Amen.

References: *(1) Psalms 46:10; (2) John 15:15; (3) Hosea 2:20; (4) Daniel 11:32; (5) Psalms 40:8; (6) 1 John 2:3; (7) Colossians 1:9-10; (8) Colossians 1:11; (9) Colossians 1:12; (10) Colossians 1:12-13; (11) Colossians 1:14-15; (12) Colossians 1:17; (13) John 10:10; (14) 1 John 1:3; (15) 2 Corinthians 13:14.*

Mental and Emotional Health

Key Thought: "God has two dwellings: one in heaven, and the other in a meek and thankful heart" (Izaak Walton).

Key Scripture: *"Keep thy heart with all diligence; for out of it are the issues of life" (Prov. 4:23).*

Prayer: Heavenly Father, I thank you that you know the secrets of the human heart,[1] and I pray that you will help my son/daughter, _____, to keep his/her heart with all diligence.[2] Help him/her to remember always that a merry heart has a continual feast,[3] and that such a heart does one good like a medicine.[4]

I pray that my son/daughter will learn how to rejoice in you always, Lord. Keep him/her from being anxious through a life of prayer and faith in you. I pray for your peace to flood his/her being, keeping his/her heart and mind through Christ Jesus.[5] Draw my son/daughter ever closer to you, Lord; let the same mind be in him/her that was in Christ Jesus, our Lord.[6]

Keep my child from all mental and emotional problems, Lord. Make him/her completely whole.[7] I ask that my son/daughter would keep your Word within his/her heart. Your teachings are life unto all who find them and health to their flesh.[8] I pray that my son/daughter will find rest in your Word, Father, and that he/she will enjoy the perfect peace you promise to those whose minds are steadfast, trusting in you.[9]

I pray that my son/daughter will experience your healing light breaking forth as the morning, and complete mental and emotional health springing forth speedily whenever problems threaten to overwhelm him/her. May your righteousness go before him/her and may your glory be his/her reward.[10]

Lord, lead _____ to offer his/her body as a living sacrifice, holy and pleasing to you as a spiritual act of worship, and to not be conformed to the pattern of this world, but to be transformed by the renewing of his/her mind, and thereby be able to know and to prove what is your good, pleasing and perfect will.[11]

Continually guide my son/daughter and satisfy his/her soul, O Lord. As you continue your workmanship in his/her life, may he/she be like a watered garden, and like a spring of water, whose waters fail not.[12] Thank you, Father, for granting total health — emotional, mental and physical — to my son/daughter.

References: *(1) Psalms 44:21; (2) Proverbs 4:23; (3) Proverbs 15:15; (4) Proverbs 17:22; (5) Philippians 4:4-7; (6) Philippians 2:5; (7) John 7:23; (8) Proverbs 4:20-24; (9) Isaiah 26:3, NIV; (10) Isaiah 58:8; (11) Romans 12:1-2, NIV; (12) Isaiah 58:11.*

My Child

Key Thought: Children need models rather than critics.

Key Scripture: *"Train up a child in the way he should go: and when he is old, he will not depart from it" (Prov. 22:6).*

Prayer: Lord God in heaven, I thank you for the precious child you have given to me, _____.
Help me to be a joyful parent to him/her.[1] My heart is full of thanksgiving and joy when I realize that my child is a gift from you — a wonderful reward from you.[2] Help me always to cherish _____ as an inheritance I have received from you, Lord.

My child is not my possession, Father. He/she is a person you have created for your specific purposes. He/she is fearfully and wonderfully made and, therefore, I will praise you because all your works are marvelous.[3]

Keep me from ever provoking my child to wrath, but help me always to remember your mandate to bring him/her up in your nurture and admonition, Lord.[4]

Keep my child from evil, Father,[5] and give your angels charge over him/her.[6] Protect him/her and lead him/her in the paths of righteousness for your name's sake.[7] Help my child to remember you in the days of his/her youth, while the evil days are not near.[8] May he/she always be an example of a believer in every way.[9]

I bless my child, Lord, even as you blessed the little children who came to you.[10] Keep him/her in the center of your will. Help him/her to discover your calling at an early age as he/she surrenders his/her will to you and trusts you for salvation and eternal life.[11]

Help me also, Lord, to discover your calling on his/her life so that the training[12] I provide for him/her will always contribute to the fulfillment of the purposes for which you created him/her.[13] Help us both to comprehend that he/she is your workmanship, created in Christ Jesus unto good works which you have ordained for him/her to walk in,[14] and that it is as _____ finds and walks in those works that he/she will experience true joy, fulfillment and blessing.[15]

May my rejoicing always be centered on the trust that my child will always walk in the truth[16] because this is your commandment. Indeed, you are the way, the truth and the life, Lord Jesus, and no one can come to the Father except through you.[17] Help my child, _____ _____, to realize this all the days of his/her life.

References: *(1) Psalms 113:9; (2) Psalms 127:3; (3) Psalms 139:14; (4) Ephesians 6:4; (5) John 17:15; (6) Psalms 91:11; (7) Psalms 23:3; (8) Ecclesiastes 12:1; (9) 1 Timothy 4:12; (10) Matthew 19:14; (11) John 3:16; (12) Proverbs 22:6; (13) Jeremiah 29:11, NIV; (14) Ephesians 2:10; (15) John 13:17; (16) 2 John 4; (17) John 14:6.*

My Daughter's Future Husband

Key Thought: "A Christian is the gentlest of men; but then he is a man" (Charles Haddon Spurgeon).

Key Scripture: *"Nevertheless, to avoid fornication, let every man have his own wife, and let every woman have her own husband. Let the husband render unto the wife due benevolence: and likewise also the wife unto the husband" (1 Cor. 7:2-3).*

Prayer: Dear God of glory, I come to you in prayer to beseech you to lead my daughter, _____ _____, to the husband you have selected for her in your perfect way[1] and your perfect will.[2] May they never defraud each other in any way.[3] I ask, O Lord, that you would prevent my daughter from being unequally yoked with her husband.[4] Grant that they would live each for the other and both for you. Even now, I ask that you would lead my daughter's future husband to a saving knowledge of your Son, our Lord and Savior Jesus Christ.[5] Help them both to keep themselves sexually pure prior to marriage and always,[6] to begin even now to pray for each other, and once they are married, to pray for each other daily.

I pray, dear heavenly Father, that my daughter will be able to say, "One man among a thousand have I found"[7] because she will recognize that her future husband is created in the image and glory of God. At the same time,

Lord, I ask that her future husband will recognize that she is his glory,[8] and will honor her as your daughter.

Help _____ and her future husband to submit to each other in fear of you.[9] I pray that he will love her as Christ loves His Church,[10] and that he would to lay down his life in loving devotion to her.[11] Above all, I pray that their love for each other and for you would be constant — a witness to all mankind.[12]

Lord, a marriage that you put together cannot be put asunder by others.[13] I pray that my daughter's marriage will be strong. Help her marriage and family be a source of fulfillment and happiness for her throughout her life.

Grant that her future husband would truly be a man of God who properly and wisely establishes his authority in the home under your direction.[14] Teach them to pray together, to worship together and to bring up their children in your nurture and admonition.[15] Lead my daughter's future husband to realize the importance of loving, cherishing and honoring my daughter, Lord, and to understand that she is the weaker vessel.[16] I pray that he will ever rejoice in his wife.[17]

References: *(1) Psalms 18:30; (2) Luke 11:2; (3) 1 Corinthians 7:5; (4) 2 Corinthians 6:14; (5) Ephesians 2:8-9; (6) 1 Timothy 5:22; (7) Ecclesisastes 7:28; (8) 1 Corinthians 11:7; (9) Ephesians 5:21; (10) Ephesians 5:25; (11) John 15:13; (12) John 13:35; (13) Matthew 19:6; (14) Ephesians 5:23-24; (15) Ephesians 6:4; (16) 1 Peter 3:7; (17) Proverbs 5:18.*

My Son's Future Wife

Key Thought: A prudent wife is from the Lord.

Key Scripture: *"Whoso findeth a wife findeth a good thing, and obtaineth favour of the Lord" (Prov. 18:22).*

Prayer: Heavenly Father, I thank you that you have ordained marriage as the cornerstone of society. I pray for my son, _____, that you will lead him to the wife you have selected for him, and I pray that he will ever rejoice with his wife.[1] Make my son and his wife truly one flesh and united in spirit before you.[2] May they covenant to live always each for the other and both for you.

For the one who is to become his wife, I now offer this prayer. Father, bless her. Lead her to a saving knowledge of your Son, Jesus Christ our Lord.[3] Give her the grace to enable her to desire her husband only and to be able to submit to him under your Lordship.[4]

May she always be a godly and virtuous woman who is pleasing to you and is a crown to her husband.[5] May my son always recognize her to be a virtuous woman whose value is far above rubies.[6]

May she adorn herself with that meek and quiet spirit, which is of so great value in your sight, Lord,[7] and may she always respect her husband.[8]

139

Prepare her heart even now, Lord, to be a wife and mother who will always look after the needs of her home and family, a wife who is not idle.[9] I pray that she will be a wife of whom it can be said, "Many daughters have done virtuously, but thou excellest them all".[10] Prevent anyone from ever dealing treacherously with the wife of my son.[11]

When you join my son to his future wife, Father, I ask that you will so bond them together that no man will ever be able to divide them asunder.[12] May they truly become one.[13] Keep my son and his wife faithful to each other, Lord.

I ask that my son's future wife will be concerned about pleasing her husband at all times.[14] Help her to submit to my son as unto you, O Lord.[15] As the Church is subject to Jesus Christ, I pray that my son's future wife will be subject unto her husband.[16] At the same time, Father, I ask that you will so fill my son that he will be able to love his wife as Christ has loved the Church.[17]

Remind my son that he who loves his wife actually loves himself.[18] May he never be bitter against her.[19] Guide _____ to always give honor to his wife as the weaker vessel, realizing that she is your daughter, and that together they are heirs of the grace of life.[20] Help them both to keep themselves sexually pure prior to marriage and always,[21] to begin even now to pray for each other, and once they are married to pray together daily. Reveal your will about a life partner to my son and help him to obey you in this important matter as in all others.

References: *(1) Proverbs 5:18; (2) Genesis 2:24; (3) John 3:16; (4) Genesis 3:16; (5) Proverbs 12:4; (6) Proverbs 31:10; (7) 1 Peter 3:4; (8) Ephesians 5:33, NIV; (9) Proverbs 31:27; (10) Proverbs 31:29 (11) Malachi 2:15; (12) Matthew 19:6; (13) Mark 10:8; (14) 1 Corinthians 7:34; (15) Ephesians 5:22; (16) Ephesians 5:24; (17) Ephesians 5:25; (18) Ephesians 5:28; (19) Colossians 3:19; (20) 1 Peter 3:7; (21) 1 Timothy 5:22.*

My Teenager

Key Thought: Cherish your teenager for whom he or she is, not for whom you want him/her to become.

Key Scripture: *"Wherewithal shall a young man cleanse his way? by taking heed thereto according to thy word. With my whole heart have I sought thee: O let me not wander from thy commandments. Thy word have I hid in mine heart, that I might not sin against thee" (Ps. 119:9-11).*

Prayer: Dear Father in heaven, I come to you now in behalf of my teenager, _____. He/she needs your unfailing love,[1] your wisdom[2] and your guidance.[3] Thank you for your willingness to supply all his/her needs according to your riches in glory.[4] Lord, supply those needs in the power of your might.[5]

Keep and protect him/her from the evil one.[6] Convict _____ of his/her need for you at all times. Draw him/her to abundant life in you.[7] How I praise and thank you, Father, that you have a plan and a purpose for his/her life.[8] Reveal your will to him/her.[9]

Help _____ to honor and remember you in the days of his/her youth, before the days of trouble come as years go by.[10] Thank you, Lord, for being the Guide of our youths.[11] I pray for young people in general, and for my teenager, _____, that they would find you early and be set free from the prevailing philosophies and behaviors of our day.[12] Father, may _____ always grow up in you in all things.[13] Help him/her to learn your ways,[14] because your ways are perfect and your Word is true.[15] Lead him/her in the paths of righteousness for your name's sake.[16] May he/she always remember that the fear (respect, reverence) of the Lord is the beginning of all wisdom.[17]

Teach _____ to keep his/her way clean by taking heed to your Word, and to hide your Word in his/her heart so that he/she might not sin against you. Encourage and strengthen him/her to seek you with his/her whole heart and not to wander from your commandments.[18]

Bring Christian friends to _____ who will encourage him/her in his/her walk with you. Prevent him/her from being tossed to and fro, and carried about with every wind of doctrine, by the sleight of men, and cunning craftiness.[19]

May his/her greatest desire always be to know you and to follow in your steps, Lord.[20] Bless him/her and use him/her to bring glory to your name.

References: (1) *1 John 4:16;* (2) *2 Chronicles 1:10;* (3) *Psalms 32:8;* (4) *Philippians 4:19;* (5) *Revelation 7:12;* (6) *Matthew 6:13;* (7) *John 10:10;* (8) *Jeremiah 29:11;* (9) *Psalms 40:8;* (10) *Ecclesiastes 12:1;* (11) *Jeremiah 3:4;* (12) *Colossians 2:8;* (13) *Ephesians 4:15;* (14) *Isaiah 2:3;* (15) *Psalms 18:30;* (16) *Psalms 23:3;* (17) *Psalms 111:10;* (18) *Psalms 119:10-11;* (19) *Ephesians 4:14;* (20) *1 Peter 2:21.*

A Newborn Baby

Key Thought: An infant's laugh is praise to God.

Key Scripture: *"And said unto him, Hearest thou what these say? And Jesus saith unto them, Yea; have ye never read, Out of the mouth of babes and sucklings thou hast perfected praise?" (Matt. 21:16).*

Prayer: Heavenly Father, I thank you and praise you for the tiny bundle of your great love you have sent to us in the form of our baby, _____.
Watch over him/her, Lord, to build, plant and establish him/her in your love.[1] Make his/her way secure,[2] and let neither evil nor plague befall him/her throughout the coming years. Give your angels charge over him/her, to keep my baby in all your ways. May his/her guardian angel bear him/her up in his hands, lest he/she should dash his/her foot against a stone. Set your love upon him/her, Lord God.[3]

Give me wisdom, Father, as I endeavor to train my baby in the way that he/she should go. By applying your wisdom to my parenting, I know that my child will not depart from your ways when he/she is older.[4] Thank you for this prevailing promise from your Word.

Your wonderful Word also declares that when I lack wisdom, I can come to you, Lord, with the full knowledge

144

that you give to all liberally. When we ask you for wisdom (if we ask in faith), it shall be given to us.[5] Thank you, Father, for this precious prayer promise. In the age in which we live, I know I will need your wisdom at all times in order to be the most effective parent I can possibly be. Help me to cherish my child always as your precious gift to me, to pray for him/her without ceasing,[6] to bring him/her up in your nurture and admonition,[7] and to always be an example to him/her in word, in conversation, in charity, in spirit, in faith, in purity.[8]

I pray for him/her to be physically healthy and strong,[9] to be mentally alert and talented,[10] and to be spiritually stalwart.[11] I also pray that when he/she lies down, he/she will have no fear and his/her sleep will be sweet.[12]

Thank you for blessing my baby, Lord, with every spiritual blessing in heavenly places in Christ. You have chosen him/her before the foundation of the world, that he/she should be holy and without blame before you in love.[13] Draw him/her to a saving knowledge of your Son, that he/she should live his/her life to the praise of your glory because he/she will place his/her trust in Christ.[14]

References: *(1) Jeremiah 31:28; (2) Job 11:18; (3) Psalms 91:10-12; (4) Proverbs 22:6; (5) James 1:5-6; (6) 1 Thessalonians 5:17; (7) Ephesians 6:4; (8) 1 Timothy 4:12; (9) 3 John 2; (10) Daniel 1:17; (11) 1 Corinthians 15:58; (12) Proverbs 3:24; (13) Ephesians 1:3; (14) Ephesians 1:12.*

Parental Wisdom

Key Thought: "The greatest good is wisdom" (Augustine).

Key Scripture: *"If any of you lack wisdom, let him ask of God, that giveth to all men liberally, and upbraideth not; and it shall be given him. But let him ask in faith, nothing wavering. For he that wavereth is like a wave of the sea driven with the wind and tossed" (James 1:5-6).*

Prayer: Dear Lord, our loving Father, I beseech you now for wisdom to enable me to be the most effective parent I can possibly be. I need you wisdom, Father, as I endeavor to make daily decisions regarding the discipline and nurture of my children. Help me at all times to be conscious of my need to bring them up in your nurture and admonition.[1]

I thank you for your Word which imparts wisdom to my spirit. I enter your presence with trust, knowing that you are giving me wisdom.[2] Your wisdom is pure, peaceable, gentle and easy to be entreated. It is full of mercy and good fruits and it does not show partiality. How I praise you that your wisdom is so different from that of the world.[3]

Fill me with the spirit of wisdom that I might discern your will, Father, when it comes to making decisions that affect the future and well-being of my child.[4] With you,

Lord, I have strength and wisdom.[5] Let my mouth speak wisdom, Lord, because of the righteousness you have imparted unto me.[6] In the hidden parts of my life, make me to know wisdom.[7] Lord, help me to apply my heart unto your wisdom.[8]

Your wisdom makes me happy, Lord, because the gain of it is better than fine gold. By wisdom you founded the earth and by knowledge you established the heavens.[9] In Jesus Christ, my Lord, I am put in touch with your wisdom and power. He has been made wisdom, righteousness, sanctification and redemption unto me. The knowledge of this causes me to glory in you forever, Father.[10]

Keep me from reacting rashly to my child and to the situations that affect him/her. Instead, help me, Father, to take positive action only after I have sought your wisdom which is more precious than rubies.[11]

References: *(1) Ephesians 6:4; (2) 2 Chronicles 1:10; (3) James 3:15-17; (4) Exodus 28:3; (5) Job 12:13; (6) Psalms 37:30; (7) Psalms 51:6; (8) Psalms 90:12; (9) Proverbs 3:13-20; (10) 1 Corinthians 1:22-31; (11) Proverbs 3:15.*

A Parent's Prayer

Key Thought: Parenting is a responsibility that counts for all eternity.

Key Scripture: *"Lo, children are an heritage of the Lord: and the fruit of the womb is his reward. As arrows are in the hand of a mighty man; so are children of the youth. Happy is the man that hath his quiver full of them" (Ps. 127:3-5).*

Prayer: Lord God, I thank you so much for my children. They are a true blessing and a rich treasure to me. Help me always to value them in the same way you value them, for of such is the kingdom of heaven.[1]

I commit myself to the important responsibility of training my children in the way they should go. Lord, I know that if I will do this faithfully, my children will not depart from my training and your guidance when they are older.[2] May they always delight to do your will, O God.[3]

Bring them to full salvation through faith in Jesus Christ, Father.[4] May I ever live in such a way that they would be attracted to your Son through me.

Father, you are my Father and you show me how a parent should nurture and care for his/her children.[5] Thank you for giving me your example and your Word to guide me as a parent in these difficult times.[6]

Lord, let me be a loving parent who seeks to understand his/her children. Let the emphasis of my relationship with my children be upon caring instead of controlling. May I become my children's safe place, Lord, even as you are my refuge,[7] my high tower,[8] my sure defense.[9]

Teach me how to manage my home well, having children who are obedient and respectful,[10] but never provoking them to anger or to wrath.[11] Help me to be fair with my children and to understand them even as you understand and love me.[12] Turn my heart to my children, and the hearts of my children to me,[13] so that our home may be blessed.

References: *(1) Luke 18:16; (2) Proverbs 22:6; (3) Psalms 40:8; (4) Ephesians 4:5; (5) Ephesians 6:4; (6) Psalms 119:105; (7) Psalms 46:1; (8) Psalms 144:2; (9) Psalms 59:17; (10) 1 Timothy 3:4, NIV; (11) Ephesians 6:4; (12) Psalms 139:23; (13) Malachi 4:6.*

Physical Health and Well-being

Key Thought: God wants your children to prosper and to be in good health.

Key Scripture: *"But unto you that fear my name shall the Sun of righteousness arise with healing in his wings"* (Mal. 4:2).

Prayer: Loving God, our heavenly Father, you are the Lord who heals.[1] With the stripes of Jesus we are healed.[2] I thank you that you do heal the broken in heart, and you bind up all our wounds.[3]

Because of who you are, I am able to come to you with confidence now in behalf of my child,[4] _____. I ask you, Lord, to keep him/her in the shadow of your almighty power.[5] Cover him/her with your feathers.[6] Give your angels charge over him/her, to keep him/her in all your ways,[7] because I know this will be health to him/her.[8]

When illness threatens, I pray that my child will remember to turn to you, to trust you with all his/her heart and to acknowledge you.[9] I thank you that the prayer of faith will save the sick, and you, Lord, will raise him/her up.[10]

I pray not only for my child's physical well-being but also for his/her emotional and mental health. I believe you want him/her to walk in wholeness, and I pray that you will make him/her completely whole through the power of your might.[11] Should he/she suffer any wounds in the inner person, I ask you to fulfill your promise by restoring health and healing those wounds.[12]

Help my son/daughter to practice good habits of exercise,[13] nutrition[14] and preventive medicine. Keep his/her heart merry and joyful, for I know that the happiness you impart is health and healing to us.[15]

Father, I ask you in the name of Jesus, to help _____ _____ always to attend to your words, incline his/her ear unto your sayings, and keep them before his/her eyes and in the midst of his/her heart, for they are life to all that find them and health and medicine to their whole body.[16]

My faith reaches out to you, Lord, in behalf of _____ _____. Because I know you to be a Rewarder to all those who come to you in faith,[17] I now express my faith to you that you will prosper my son/daughter and keep his/her body and soul in good health.[18] Lord, keep his/her way secure.[19]

References: *(1) Psalms 103:3; (2) Isaiah 53:5; (3) Isaiah 61:1; (4) Hebrews 4:16; (5) Psalms 91:1; (6) Psalms 91:4; (7) Psalms 91:11; (8) Proverbs 3:8; (9) Proverbs 3:5-6; (10) James 5:15; (11) Matthew 9:22; (12) Jeremiah 30:17; (13) 1 Timothy 4:8; (14) Genesis 50:21; (15) Proverbs 17:22; (16) Proverbs 4:20-22; (17) Hebrews 11:6; (18) 3 John 2; (19) Job 11:18.*

The Power of Prayer

Key Thought: "Prayer is a strong wall and fortress of the Church" (Martin Luther).

Key Scripture: *"Our Father which art in heaven, Hallowed be thy name. Thy kingdom come. Thy will be done in earth, as it is in heaven" (Matt. 6:9-10).*

Prayer: Father, I thank you for the direct access we have to you through prayer. I pray that my son/daughter, _____ , will understand the importance of prayer and will be diligent to pray daily.

Show him/her that if he/she will ask, you will answer. Reveal to him/her that if he/she will seek, he/she will find, and if he/she will knock, you will open the door for him/her.[1] Lead him/her to know you so well, Father, that he/she will realize that you always give good things to those who ask you,[2] and that you love to reward those who diligently seek you.[3]

Where two or three are gathered together in the name of Jesus Christ, your Son, you have promised to be in the midst of them.[4] Thank you, Father, for all the rich and precious prayer promises of your Word. Help my son/daughter to appropriate these into his/her life and to know that all of your promises are yes in Christ.[5]

Teach my son/daughter to believe in you with all his/her heart so that whatsoever he/she shall ask in prayer, believing, he/she shall receive.[6] When he/she prays, help him/her to forgive any and all that he/she has anything against so that you can forgive his/her trespasses.[7]

As my son/daughter learns to trust you for the answers to his/her prayers, I pray that he/she will exercise the necessary faith to receive your answers so that his/her joy will be full.[8] By prayer and supplication with thanksgiving, I ask that he/she would let his/her requests be made known unto you, dear Lord.[9]

May he/she become a true prayer warrior and intercessor in your army, Lord. Teach him/her (and myself) to pray without ceasing,[10] to ask in faith without wavering,[11] and to always pray the prayer of faith.[12]

Teach him/her that the effectual, fervent prayer of a righteous person will avail much,[13] and the eyes of the Lord are over the righteous and His ears are open unto their prayers.[14] How I praise you and thank you, Father, for the certainty of your promise that if we pray according to your will you will always hear us, and that because you hear us, we then shall have the petitions we have asked of you.[15] Show _____ the power of this promise, O Lord.

References: *(1) Matthew 7:7; (2) Matthew 7:11; (3) Hebrews 11:6; (4) Matthew 18:20; (5) 2 Corinthians 1:20; (6) Matthew 21:22; (7) Mark 11:25; (8) John 16:24; (9) Philippians 4:6; (10) 1 Thessalonians 5:17; (11) James 1:6; (12) James 5:15; (13) James 5:16; (14) 1 Peter 3:12; (15) 1 John 5:14-15.*

A Prosperous Future

Key Thought: "Prayer is the golden key that opens heaven" (Thomas Watson).

Key Scripture: *"And he shall be like a tree planted by the rivers of water, that bringeth forth his fruit in his season; his leaf also shall not wither; and whatsoever he doeth shall prosper" (Ps. 1:3).*

Prayer: Heavenly Father, I thank you that you shower your blessings upon your children.[1] You do not withhold any good thing from those who love you and walk uprightly. I pray for my child, Lord, that you would be his/her sun and shield. Give your grace and glory to _____ and shower your blessings upon him/her.[2] Help my son/daughter to learn the importance of placing his/her full and uncompromising trust in you for you are the Lord of hosts, and every person who trusts in you is blessed.[3]

Equip _____ with success by leading him/her to meditate upon your Word both night and day and to observe to do all that your Word declares so that he/she will enjoy prosperity and success.[4] Teach him/her to be faithful in all his/her responsibilities. Your Word teaches that a faithful person will abound with your blessings,[5] Lord. I pray that my child will be full of faith and wisdom as your servant Stephen was.[6]

My prayer for my son/daughter is and will always be that at the end of his/her life on earth you will say to him/her: "Well done, good and faithful servant: you have been faithful over a few things, I will make you ruler over many things: enter into the joy of your Lord."[7] Lord, I know that your measurement of success and prosperity is the only one that counts.

Help my child to fulfill your will, Father, and to realize that you measure successful living by whether he/she loves you with all his/her heart, and his/her neighbor as well.[8] Help him/her to endeavor to owe no one anything, but love, and to realize that he who loves has fulfilled your law.[9] Help me to be an example of all these things to my son/daughter.

Give _____ the desire to hearken unto your voice and obey your commands so that all your blessings shall overtake him/her.[10] Lord, you know the plans you have for him/her, plans to prosper him/her and not to harm him/her, plans to give him/her a hope and a future. I pray that _____ will call upon you and seek you with all his/her heart, and that you will reveal the plans you have for his/her future.[11]

References: *(1) Ezekiel 34:26; (2) Psalms 84:11; (3) Psalms 84:12; (4) Joshua 1:8; (5) Proverbs 28:20; (6) Acts 6:5; (7) Matthew 25:21-23; (8) Galatians 5:14; (9) Romans 13:8; (10) Deuteronomy 28:1-2; (11) Jeremiah 29:11-13, NIV.*

Protection During Temptation

Key Thought: "Temptation provokes me to look upward to God" (John Bunyan).

Key Scripture: *"Blessed is the man that endureth temptation; for when he is tried, he shall receive the crown of life, which the Lord hath promised to them that love him" (James 1:12).*

Prayer: Heavenly Father, I thank you for the promises of your Word. You have revealed to us that no temptation will come to us that is different from the temptations that are common to others. I believe your Word, Father, and I come to you now in behalf of my son/daughter, _____ _____ , asking that you will never permit him/her to be tempted above his/her ability to resist the temptation. Lord, always provide a way for him/her to escape the temptations that come, and give him/her the will and the wisdom to choose your way of escape. In the certain knowledge that you will provide a way, Lord, there is peace and rest and victory that enables us to bear the temptations and the testings.[1] Thank you, Lord.

I praise you that you cannot be tempted with evil, Lord, and you never tempt your people.[2] Protect my son/daughter from the temptations that the enemy puts in his/her way. Empower him/her through your Spirit and your Word to resist all temptations in the same way your

Son, our Lord and Savior Jesus Christ, resisted the enemy's temptations while He was on earth.[3] Show _____ that the enemy always flees when the Word of God is used to confront him because your Word, O Father, is the sword of the Spirit.[4]

Help _____ to always remember that your Word, hidden in his/her heart, will help to keep him/her from sin.[5] Give him/her the grace to follow your command, "Submit yourselves therefore to God. Resist the devil, and he will flee from you. Draw nigh to God, and he will draw nigh to you."[6] Teach _____ _____ to live and walk by the leading of your Holy Spirit and thereby not gratify the lusts of the flesh.[7]

I realize, Lord, that I cannot pray that no temptations will come to my child, but I do pray that you will keep him/her from falling victim to the schemes of Satan. Lead him/her not into temptation and deliver him/her from all evil and the evil one.[8] Whenever my son/daughter sins, I ask, Lord, that you will remind him/her that he/she has an Advocate with you who is Jesus Christ.[9] Tell him/her to confess his/her sins so that you can forgive him/her and cleanse him/her from all unrighteousness. Thank you, Lord, for leading him/her and helping him/her to lean on you.[10]

References: *(1) 1 Corinthians 10:13; (2) James 1:13; (3) Matthew 4:1-11; (4) Ephesians 6:17; (5) Psalms 119:11; (6) James 4:7-8; (7) Galatians 5:16; (8) Matthew 6:13; (9) 1 John 2:1; (10) 1 John 1:9.*

Protection From Evil

Key Thought: "All that is necessary for the triumph of evil is that good men do nothing" (Edmund Burke).

Key Scripture: *"And unto man he said, Behold, the fear of the Lord, that is wisdom; and to depart from evil is understanding" (Job 28:28).*

Prayer: Father God, Lord of lords, I come to you now in behalf of my son/daughter, _____.
I implore you to protect him/her from all evil, to deliver him/her from evil[1] when it comes near, and to lead him/her to depart from all evil[2] at all times. Keep him/her from evil always, Lord, so that you will not be grieved.[3] There is so much evidence around us, Father, that the imagination of our hearts is evil from our youth;[4] eradicate all vestiges of an evil imagination from _____ _____ as he/she learns to place his/her total trust in you,[5] and to take all thoughts captive, making them obedient to Christ.[6]

Teach _____ to abide in you,[7] and to hate evil,[8] to avoid it, pass by it, turn from it, and depart from it[9] throughout his/her life.

Give my son/daughter perception and discernment[10] through your Spirit and your Word[11] that will enable him/her always to know the difference between right and wrong and to always choose the right.[12] Give him/her a healthy fear (respect, reverence, awe) for you so that he/she will always hate evil[13] as you hate it, Lord.

Keep _____ from yielding to temptation and deliver him/her from evil and the evil one.[14] Let him/her always love the light rather than the darkness so that he/she will be able to walk in the light as you are in the light.[15] May he/she always realize that everyone who does evil hates the light.[16]

Keep my son/daughter pure, Lord.[17] I ask that he/she would always remember that bad company corrupts good character,[18] and that in order to maintain a good reputation, he/she must avoid the very appearance of evil.[19] Show him/her, Father, that the love of money is the root of all evil,[20] and that the tongue is a fire, a world of iniquity.[21]

Keep _____ ever conscious that in order to love life and see good days, he/she must refrain his/her tongue from all evil,[22] including gossip, slander, and profanity. Teach him/her that a wholesome tongue is a tree of life.[23]

Thank you for protecting my son/daughter from all evil throughout his/her life.

References: (1) Matthew 6:13; (2) Job 28:28; (3) 1 Chronicles 4:10; (4) Genesis 8:21; (5) Proverbs 3:5; (6) 2 Corinthians 10:5; (7) John 15:4; (8) Proverbs 8:13; (9) Proverbs 4:15; (10) Ecclesiastes 8:5; (11) Hebrews 4:12; (12) Proverbs 20:11; (13) Proverbs 8:13; (14) Luke 11:4; (15) 1 John 1:7; (16) John 3:19; (17) 1 John 3:3; (18) 1 Corinthians 15:33, NIV; (19) 1 Thessalonians 5:22; (20) 1 Timothy 6:10; (21) James 3:6; (22) 1 Peter 3:10; (23) Proverbs 15:4.

Protection From Evildoers

Key Thought: God's protection cannot fail.

Key Scripture: *"Because thou hast made the Lord, which is my refuge, even the most High, thy habitation; There shall no evil befall thee, neither shall any plague come nigh thy dwelling" (Ps. 91:9-10).*

Prayer: King of kings and Lord of lords, I enter your presence now[1] in behalf of my son/daughter, _____ _____. I pray, Father, that your strong arm will always protect him/her from all evildoers.[2]

I thank you that you will never justify the wicked.[3] You know how people are set on mischief,[4] and the thoughts of the wicked are an abomination to you.[5] Keep my son/daughter from evildoers, Father.[6]

Help _____ not to fret because of evildoers.[7] Let him/her see that all evildoers will be cut down like the grass, and wither as the green herb does.[8] Instead, Lord, I pray that _____ will be focused on trusting in you and doing good. May he/she ever delight in you, Master, and in so doing realize the desires of his/her heart.[9] Empower my son/daughter to commit his/her way unto you, to rest in you and wait patiently for you whenever workers of iniquity come near. Keep him/her from all worry as he she realizes that evil-

doers will be cut off by you and from you, O Lord.[10] Let
_____ understand that the meek
will inherit the earth and shall delight themselves in the
abundance of peace.[11]

Whenever my son/daughter sees the wicked plotting
against the just, perhaps even against himself/herself, I
pray that he/she will remember that you, Lord, know all
things, that vengeance is yours, that you will repay the
evildoers,[12] and that the wicked will perish.[13] I thank you,
Lord, for the knowledge that your enemies will be as the
fat of lambs; they shall consume — into smoke shall they
consume away.[14]

I pray that no weapon that is formed against my
son/daughter will prosper, and that every tongue that shall
rise against him/her in judgment shall be condemned, for
this is the heritage of your servants, Lord.[15]

Teach my son/daughter to wait on you, O Lord, and
to keep his/her way. As he/she does so, reveal the truth to
him/her and assure him/her that you will exalt him/her to
inherit the land, and he/she will live to see the wicked cut
off.[16] Ever remind _____that you
are his/her strength in the time of trouble.[17] You will
always help him/her and deliver him/her. I thank you,
Father, that you will deliver him/her from the wicked.
You will save him/her because he/she has learned to trust
implicitly and unreservedly in you.[18]

References: *(1) Psalms 100:2; (2) Jeremiah 21:5; (3) Exodus
23:7; (4) Exodus 32:22; (5) Proverbs 15:26; (6) Psalms 37:9;
(7) Psalms 37:7; (8) Psalms 37:2; (9) Psalms 37:4 ; (10) Psalms
37:9; (11) Psalms 37:11; (12) Romans 12:19; (13) Psalms*

37:20; (14) Psalms 37:20; (15) Isaiah 54:17; (16) Psalms 37:28; (17) Psalms 37:39; (18) Psalms 37:40.

Protection From Negative Influences

Key Thought: Jesus turns negative influences into positive opportunities.

Key Scripture: *"To open their eyes, and to turn them from darkness to light, and from the power of Satan unto God, that they may receive forgiveness of sins, and inheritance among them which are sanctified by faith that is in me" (Acts 26:18).*

Prayer: Father of lights, in whom there is no variableness or shadow of turning, I come to you now, asking that you would send enlightenment to my son/daughter, _____ _____.[1] May he/she ever walk in the light of your Word,[2] and may he/she always take heed that the light that is in him/her never be darkened.[3] Your light shines in the darkness, Father, and the darkness cannot comprehend it,[4] but all those who receive your Son, the Lord Jesus Christ, are given the power to become your children.[5] I pray, Father, that _____ would receive Jesus as his/her personal Savior and Lord, that he/she would always walk with Jesus[6] and keep His light shining for the world to see.

Protect _____ from all negative influences that will attempt to distract him/her from all that you have for him/her. Protect him/her from the negative influences of his/her peer group, the media, fallen leaders and ungodly philosophies.[7] I thank you, Lord, that you are light itself, and in you there is no darkness or negativity at all.[8]

Be a shield at all times to my son/daughter, Lord, I pray, and be his/her exceeding great reward.[9] Deliver him/her from all evil influences,[10] darkness,[11] deception,[12] despair[13] and depression[14] through hope in you.[15] Keep him/her close to you.[16] Go before my son/daughter by day and night and always give him/her your light to guide him/her.[17] Help _____ to ever trust in you, and as he/she learns to trust, I ask, O Lord, that you would be his/her buckler.[18] Deliver him/her from all enemies — especially those who would attempt to bring to bear negative influences in his/her life.[19]

Lead my son/daughter to prayer, Father, whenever negative influences attempt to assault his/her life. May his/her prayer ever be: "Be not far from me; for trouble is near; for there is none to help except you, O Lord."[20]

References: *(1) James 1:17; (2) Psalms 119:130; (3) Luke 11:35; (4) John 1:5; (5) John 1:12; (6) Colossians 2:6; (7) Colossians 2:8; (8) 1 John 1:5; (9) Genesis 15:1; (10) Genesis 32:11; (11) Acts 26:18; (12) Matthew 7:15; (13) John 6:35; (14) Psalms 69:1; (15) Psalms 42:5; (16) Psalms 121:5; (17) Exodus 13:21; (18) 2 Samuel 22:31; (19) 2 Kings 17:39; (20) Psalms 22:11.*

Protection From Satan

Key Thought: Satan can be only in one place at a time; he is not omnipresent.

Key Scripture: *"Be sober, be vigilant; because your adversary the devil, as a roaring lion, walketh about, seeking whom he may devour"* (1 Pet. 5:8).

Prayer: Dear Lord, I pray for my son/daughter, _____ _____, asking you to always remind him/her that he/she is able to overcome the enemy by the blood of the Lamb, your Son and our Savior, Jesus Christ, and by the word of his/her testimony.[1]   Prevent _____ _____ from ever being ignorant of Satan's devices.[2] I ask, dear heavenly Father, that you would enable my son/daughter to put on the whole armor you provide each day so that he/she will be able to stand against the devil's wiles.[3]

I pray that _____ will always submit to you, Lord,[4] ever resisting the devil in the full knowledge that he will flee when my son/daughter resists him in the name of Jesus Christ.[5] Keep him/her conscious of the fact that he/she is not wrestling against flesh and blood in the struggles of his/her life, but against principalities, powers and the rulers of the darkness of this world and spiritual wickedness in heavenly places.[6]

Keep my son/daughter in an attitude of alertness so that he/she will remain vigilant at all times, in the full realization that his/her enemy, the devil, walks about as a roaring lion, seeking people to devour.[7]

I thank you, Father, that the devils are subject unto us through your name.[8] You have cast the devil and his angels out of your kingdom and you have consigned them to eternal torment.[9] Help _____ to remember that Satan is a defeated foe and that the Spirit of Christ who dwells within him/her is incomparably greater than the one who is in the world.[10]

Give my son/daughter the necessary spiritual discernment to recognize the schemes of Satan, to expose them,[11] to realize that there is no truth in him,[12] because he is a liar and the father of lies.[13] Help him/her to remember that it is Satan who is the accuser of the brethren,[14] and though he comes as an angel of light, his goal is always deception, destruction and darkness.[15]

Guide him/her to cast down all evil reasonings and every high thing that would exalt itself against the knowledge of God, and to take every thought captive, bringing it into obedience to Christ.[16]

Assure _____ that no weapon that is formed against him/her shall prosper. Help him/her to realize that every tongue raised against him/her in judgment will be condemned. How I thank you, Lord, that this is the heritage of your servants and their righteousness is of you.[17]

Always enable _____ to stand fast in the liberty wherewith you have set him/her free and to never be entangled with a yoke of bondage.[18] Thank you, Father, that you will bring these things to pass in his/her life.

References: *(1) Revelation 12:11; (2) 2 Corinthians 2:11; (3) Ephesians 6:11; (4) James 4:7; (5) Mark 16:17; (6) Ephesians 6:12; (7) 1 Peter 5:8; (8) Luke 10:17; (9) John 12:31 ; (10) 1 John 4:4; (11) 1 Corinthians 4:5; (12) John 8:44; (13) John 8:44; (14) Revelation 12:10; (15) 2 Corinthians 11:14 ; (16) 2 Corinthians 10:5; (17) Isaiah 54:17; (18) Galatians 5:1.*

Protection From Sin

Key Thought: Sin separates us from God.

Key Scripture: *"There is nothing covered, that shall not be revealed; neither hid, that shall not be known" (Luke 12:2).*

Prayer: Heavenly Father, I thank you for your Word which is able to keep us from sin. Help my son/daughter, _____, to rely on your Word by hiding it in his/her heart so that he/she will not sin.[1] Let your Word be like a fire within him/her and like a hammer that would smash the appeal of the world and sin in his/her life.[2]

Lead _____ to know that his/her sin will discovered.[3] Teach him/her that the worst sin of all is to forsake you and your teachings.[4] Remember not the sins of his/her youth,[5] and show him/her that if he/she will confess his/her sins, you will forgive him/her and cleanse him/her from all unrighteousness.[6]

Thank you, Father, that where sin abounds, grace does much more abound.[7] I pray for your grace to abound in the life of _____. Thank you for laying his/her iniquities and the iniquities of all of us on your Son, our Lord and Savior Jesus Christ.[8] He is our advocate with you, Father.[9] I thank you that He who knew no sin became sin for us.[10]

Show my son/daughter that whatsoever is not of faith is sin.[11] Lead him/her to believe in you with all his/her heart so that he/she will always be able to receive remission of his/her sins.[12] Help him/her to put on the Lord Jesus Christ and to make no provision for the flesh, to fulfill its lusts.[13]

Protect him/her from sin, Father, and from all the lures of this world, the lusts of the flesh and the schemes of Satan. Let the blood of Jesus Christ, your Son, cleanse him/her from all sin as he/she walks in your light.[14] May your constant love cover the sins in his/her life.[15] I pray, Father, that my son/daughter will realize that to him that knows to do good but does not do it, to him it is sin.[16] I ask that _____ will always strive to do what is good.

Protect my son/daughter from the gall of bitterness and the bonds of iniquity.[17] When his/her spirit is willing to follow your will, but his/her flesh is weak, I pray that you will protect him/her from sin.[18] Guide him/her to obey your Word and reckon himself/herself to be dead to sin, but alive to you, O God, through the Lord Jesus Christ.[19]

References: (1) Psalms 119:9-11; (2) Jeremiah 23:29; (3) Numbers 32:23; (4) 1 Samuel 12:10; (5) Psalms 25:7; (6) 1 John 1:9; (7) Romans 5:20; (8) Isaiah 53:6; (9) 1 John 2:1; (10) 2 Corinthians 5:21; (11) Romans 14:23; (12) Acts 10:43; (13) Romans 13:14; (14) 1 John 1:7; (15) 1 Peter 4:8; (16) James 4:17; (17) Acts 8:23; (18) Matthew 26:41; (19) Romans 6:11.

Protection From Wrong Thinking

Key Thought: The gap between God's thoughts and our thoughts is bridged by faith in His Word.

Key Scripture: *"For my thoughts are not your thoughts, neither are your ways my ways, saith the Lord. For as the heavens are higher than the earth, so are my ways higher than your ways, and my thoughts than your thoughts"* *(Isa. 55:8-9).*

Prayer: Loving Father, I thank you for the intellectual capacities you have given to my son/daughter, _____ _____. Help him/her to think clearly at all times, to line up his/her thoughts with yours by thinking on things that are true, honest, just, pure, lovely, and of good report.[1] Let the mind that was in Christ Jesus our Lord be in him/her, O God.[2] Lead him/her to continually renew his/her mind through your Word,[3] so that he/she will not be conformed to this world.[4] Guide him/her to put on the new man who is created for righteousness and true holiness.[5]

Lead him/her to use his/her mind to further your kingdom on earth, Lord.[6] Help him/her to discern between right and wrong, to know your will and to realize that a person is greatly influenced by whatever he/she thinks in his/her heart.[7] Remind him/her that you alone know the hearts of all the children of men.[8] You have pointed out that most of the thoughts of our hearts are vanity.[9] There is not a word on our tongues that you do not know before we speak it.[10] Show _____ that the thoughts of the wicked are an abomination to you.[11] You know everything that comes into our minds.[12]

In light of all these truths declared in your Word, Father, I pray that you will reveal to my son/daughter the importance of always thinking soberly.[13] Help him/her to gird up the loins of his/her mind,[14] to put on the helmet of salvation,[15] and never to think more highly of himself/herself than he/she ought to think.[16]

Guide him/her to guard his/her heart with all diligence, remembering that the issues of life stem from the heart.[17] Comfort him/her with the realization that your plans for him/her are plans of prosperity, not of harm, to give him/her hope and a future.[18] Show him/her that if he/she will seek you with all his/her heart, you will be found.[19] Thank you, Father.

References: *(1) Philippians 4:8; (2) Philippians 2:5; (3) Ephesians 4:23; (4) Romans 12:2; (5) Ephesians 4:24; (6) Luke 11:2; (7) Proverbs 23:7; (8) 1 Kings 8:39; (9) Psalms 94:11; (10) Psalms 139:4; (11) Proverbs 15:26; (12) Ezekiel 11:5; (13) Romans 12:3; (14) 1 Peter 1:13; (15) Ephesians 6:17; (16) Romans 12:3; (17) Proverbs 4:23; (18) Jeremiah 29:11, NIV; (19) Jeremiah 29:13.*

Responsibility

Key Thought: Responsibility involves our response to His ability.

Key Scripture: *"A good man out of the good treasure of the heart bringeth forth good things: and an evil man out of the evil treasure bringeth forth evil things. But I say unto you, That every idle word that men shall speak, they shall give account thereof in the day of judgment" (Matt. 12:35-36).*

Prayer: Heavenly Father, I thank you for the gifts you have so freely bestowed upon us.[1] Help me and my son/daughter, _____, to always remember that we are accountable to you for the proper use of the blessings you have bestowed upon us.[2] Give _____ wisdom, Father, so that he/she will know how to be fully responsible and accountable unto you.[3]

Give my son/daughter the grace to gird up his/her loins,[4] to put on the spiritual armor that you provide,[5] and to remember that unto whomsoever much is given, much shall be required.[6]

I pray for my son/daughter, that he/she would be faithful to his/her responsibilities to you and to all others. Show him/her that the person who is faithful in little things is someone who can be trusted with much responsibility.[7]

Let _____ always be faithful in the little things, Lord, and in the big things as well.

As a believer in your Word, Father, I pray that _____ _____ will faithfully feed your sheep and your lambs.[8] Help him/her to be like the Apostle Paul who realized that he put childish things away when he became an adult.[9] Teach him/her to fulfill the law of Christ by walking in love and bearing the burdens of other believers.[10] Help him/her to bear his/her own burden faithfully and with the strength you provide.[11]

May my son/daughter always be able to show appropriate restraint in the trying circumstances and relationships that life presents to him/her. Remind him/her, Lord, that whosoever will keep his mouth and his tongue will keep his soul from troubles.[12] Let him/her see, when the responsibilities of life threaten to overwhelm him/her, that through you he/she can accomplish all things.[13]

References: (1) Matthew 10:8; (2) Romans 14:12; (3) James 1:5; (4) Job 38:3; (5) Ephesians 6:11; (6) Luke 12:48; (7) Luke 16:10; (8) John 21:15-17; (9) 1 Corinthians 13:11; (10) Galatians 6:2; (11) Galatians 6:5; (12) Proverbs 21:23; (13) Philippians 4:13.

Safety and Protection

Key Thought: God's ark of safety protects against life's floods.

Key Scripture: *"The eternal God is thy refuge, and underneath are the everlasting arms: and he shall thrust out the enemy from before thee; and shall say, Destroy them" (Deut. 33:27).*

Prayer: Heavenly Father, you are the sure defense of our children,[1] you are their rock of refuge,[2] their high tower[3] and their protector.[4] How I praise you and thank you for the certain knowledge I have that you care for my child,[5] you will be with him/her always[6] and you will keep him/her from the evil one.[7]

Lord, you saved Israel from the hands of their enemies time and time again. You delivered your people and helped them to dwell in safety.[8] Be a very present help to my son/daughter as he/she faces the challenges and responsibilities of our society.[9]

Keep our home safe from all fear,[10] and dispatch your angels to protect my children.[11] Uphold my child, _____, according to your Word, Lord, that he/she might truly live, experiencing the abundant life you have promised to all who come to you.[12] Let him/her never be ashamed of you. Hold him/her up so that he/she will always be safe and will have respect to your statutes continually.[13] I thank you, Father, for the promises of your Word, and that you are a shield unto them that put their trust in you.[14]

Your name, O Lord, is a strong tower into which the righteous may run and find security, safety and protection.[15] Lead my son/daughter to find his/her safety in the protective tower of your name. Remind my child always that the fear of man brings a snare, but whoever places his/her trust in the Lord shall be safe.[16]

Your Word declares that anyone who hearkens unto you will dwell safely and shall be quiet from all fear of evil.[17] Lead _____ to hearken unto you early in his/her life, Lord. May all my children, grandchildren and succeeding generations always dwell safely in our land because they know you as their Lord. Break the bands of all yokes that threaten them, and deliver them from all who would do them harm. Thank you, Father, that I am able to know that they will dwell safely, free from all fear.[18]

References: *(1) Psalms 59:9; (2) Psalms 94:22; (3) Psalms 144:2; (4) Deuteronomy 32:38; (5) 1 Peter 5:7; (6) Matthew 28:20; (7) Galatians 1:4; (8) 1 Samuel 12:11; (9) Psalms 46:1; (10) Job 21:9; (11) Matthew 4:6; (12) John 10:10; (13) Psalms 119:116-117; (14) Proverbs 30:5; (15) Proverbs 18:10; (16) Proverbs 29:25; (17) Proverbs 1:33; (18) Ezekiel 34:27-28.*

The Salvation of My Child

Key Thought: Salvation is free because Jesus paid for it.

Key Scripture: *"For by grace are ye saved through faith; and that not of yourselves: it is the gift of God: Not of works, lest any man should boast" (Eph. 2:8-9).*

Prayer: Precious Lord, our Savior, I beseech you now for the salvation of my son/daughter, _____ _____. I thank you that it is not your will that any should perish but that all should come to the knowledge of your salvation.[1] I praise you, Father, that this is your will for _____ , and I believe that you will hear my prayer because I am praying according to your will.[2]

Father, I thank you for sending your Son, Jesus, to die on the cross for me, my child and for all those who come to you in faith.[3] His blood was shed to redeem us from all iniquity,[4] and to cleanse us from our sins.[5]

Thank you, Lord, for commending your love toward us in that while we were yet sinners, Christ died for us.[6] Help my son/daughter to appropriate your saving love and receive your precious gift of eternal life.[7]

Grant unto my son/daughter the gift of repentance, Father.[8] I thank you that your goodness will lead him/her to full repentance.[9] Guide him/her with your eye, Lord,[10] so that he/she will determine in his/her heart to follow you.[11]

Lead my son/daughter to acknowledge you as the Lord of his/her life.[12] May he/she never be ashamed of the Gospel of Jesus Christ for it is your power unto salvation.[13] Help him/her to proclaim the good news openly, to believe your Word, to confess with his/her mouth that Jesus is his/her Lord, and to believe in his/her heart that you raised Him from the dead, to your eternal honor and glory.[14]

References: (1) 2 Peter 3:9; (2) 1 John 5:14-15; (3) Ephesians 2:16; (4) Ephesians 1:7; (5) 1 John 1:7; (6) Romans 5:8; (7) Romans 6:23; (8) Acts 11:18; (9) Romans 2:4; (10) Psalms 32:8; (11) Luke 14:27-28; (12) Colossians 2:6; (13) Romans 1:16; (14) Romans 10:9-10.

Sexual Wholeness

Key Thought: "Purity of soul cannot be lost without consent" (Augustine).

Key Scripture: *"Finally, brethren, whatsoever things are true, whatsoever things are honest, whatsoever things are just, whatsoever things are pure, whatsoever things are lovely, whatsoever things are of good report; if there be any virtue, and if there be any praise, think on these things" (Phil. 4:8).*

Prayer: Dear God, in whom we live and move and have our being,[1] I come to you now in behalf of my son/daughter, _____ , asking you to give him/her the desire to keep sexually pure,[2] to flee youthful lusts,[3] to avoid the sins of fornication and adultery throughout his/her life[4] and to seek purity of heart at all times.[5]

Lord, our age militates against sexual purity and many young people are being deceived and confused by the spirit of the age in which we live.[6] I know this is not your will for my son/daughter, Lord. You are not the author of confusion,[7] but you are the Giver of every good and perfect gift.[8] Give insights to my son/daughter so that he/she will realize that it is the pure in heart who will see you.[9]

Help my son/daughter to see the importance of marriage which you have compared to your Son's relationship with the Church.[10] Grant him/her the grace and the will to remain chaste always. In marriage, Father, I pray that my son/daughter will find the joy of complete sexual fulfillment.

The pride of life, the lust of the flesh and the lust of the eyes are of this world, Father, and I know they are not your will for my son/daughter.[11] Keep him/her from evil,[12] and deliver him/her from all sexual deception and confusion.[13]

Help him/her to walk in the Spirit, Lord, and not to fulfill the lusts of the flesh.[14] Guide and empower him/her to follow your pathway of righteousness, faith, love and peace with all those who call upon you out of a pure heart.[15] Let the fruit of self-control[16] grow in him/her and strengthen him/her by your Spirit to put to death the deeds of the body[17] that war against the soul.[18] Teach _____ _____ how to give no place to the devil,[19] and how to take captive every thought and bring it into obedience to Christ.[20]

Thank you for the gift of human sexuality; help my son/daughter to be able to enjoy this gift in the ways you intended.

References: *(1) Acts 17:28; (2) 1 Timothy 5:22; (3) 2 Timothy 2:22; (4) 1 Thessalonians 4:3; (5) Matthew 5:8; (6) 2 John 7; (7) 1 Corinthians 14:33; (8) James 1:17; (9) Matthew 5:8; (10) Ephesians 5:22-32; (11) 1 John 2:16; (12) John 17:15; (13) Romans 8:21; (14) Galatians 5:16; (15) 2 Timothy 2:22; (16) Galatians 5:23; (17) Romans 8:13; (18) 1 Peter 2:11; (19) Ephesians 4:27; (20) 2 Corinthians 10:5.*

A Single Parent's Prayer

Key Thought: God's grace is sufficient for me.

Key Scripture: *"Our [my] help is in the name of the Lord, who made heaven and earth" (Ps. 124:8).*

Prayer: O God, I come before your throne confidently in order to receive mercy and grace to help in my time of need.[1] It is not easy to be a single parent, Father, but knowing that you are a very present help to me at all times gives me a feeling of great comfort and security.[2]

Lord God, you are so great, and you are greatly to be praised.[3] You will be my God forever.[4]

As I call upon you, I know you will deliver me. I will always glorify you.[5] Your promises are so beautiful to me.

Yes, I do at times feel lonely, Lord, but I know you hear my cry. You always attend to my prayer.[6] When my heart is overwhelmed, you lead me to the rock that is higher than I.[7]

Thank you, Father, for my child, _____ _____. I realize that he/she is a wonderful heritage you have given to me. I accept him/her as a reward from your hands.[8]

You have promised, Lord, to be a parent to my child and to me.[9] Thank you for sharing the parental responsibilities with me and for showing me how to be an effective parent. You set the solitary in families.[10] Thank you for being a part of our family, Lord. You protect us, provide for us and watch out for us.

You, Lord, are my helper, and I will not fear what man shall do unto me.[11] Lord, you are the same yesterday, today and forever.[12] I cast all my care on you, for I know you care for me.[13]

Instead of fretting and worrying, Lord, I want to learn to trust you with all my heart. Help me to be like Mary who chose what is better, knowing that it will not be taken away from me.[14]

Father, I ask for the patience and wisdom I need to parent my child properly, for you give liberally to all who ask of you.[15] Thank you for your promise that as I trust in you with all my heart, and lean not to my own understanding, but in all my ways acknowledge you, that you will direct my paths.[16] I praise you that you are my Shepherd,[17] you are my Helper and you will never leave me nor forsake me.[18]

I want to learn how not to worry about the needs of my life, what I shall eat, or what I shall drink; or what I shall wear.[19] I trust you to keep me from all worry about being a single parent and to teach me how to be content (through your love and peace) in the present circumstances of my life.[20] I know you will supply all our needs in your perfect way and in your perfect timing.[21] Thank you, Father.

in your perfect way and in your perfect timing.[21] Thank you, Father.

References: *(1) Hebrews 4:16; (2) Psalms 46:1; (3) Psalms 48:1; (4) Psalms 48:14; (5) Psalms 50:15; (6) Psalms 61:1-2; (7) Psalms 61:2; (8) Psalms 127:3; (9) Psalms 68:5; (10) Psalms 68:6; (11) Hebrews 13:6; (12) Hebrews 13:8; (13) 1 Peter 5:7; (14) Luke 10:42; (15) James 1:5; (16) Proverbs 3:5-6; (17) Psalms 23:1; (18) Hebrews 13:5-6; (19) Matthew 6:25-34; (20) Philippians 4:11; (21) Philippians 4:19.*

Spirituality

Key Thought: Spirit first; all else last.

Key Scripture: *"Lay up for yourselves treasures in heaven, where neither moth nor rust doth corrupt, and where thieves do not break through nor steal" (Matt. 6:20).*

Prayer: Father, I thank you that true spirituality is a matter of the heart. The natural man does not know the things of your Spirit because they are spiritually discerned.[1] I pray for my son/daughter, _____ _____, asking you, O Lord, to keep the primary focus of his/her heart on spirituality and godliness rather than temporal or natural things. Keep a watch on his/her heart, Father, and always convict him/her of sin and his/her need of loving and following you with all his/her heart, mind, soul and strength.[2]

Teach _____ that man does not live by bread alone, but by every word that proceeds from your mouth.[3] In your light, O Lord, he/she will see light — the light of your Word.[4] I thank you for the realization that your Word will be a light unto his/her path and a lamp unto his/her feet.[5] Keep your light shining in his/her life, Lord, and guide him/her into all truth.[6]

Create in him/her a clean heart, O God; and keep on renewing a right spirit within him/her.[7] I pray that the

theme of _____'s life will always be
to seek you, your kingdom priorities and your righteousness first, realizing that by so doing you will provide all
things for him/her.[8] Keep him/her from all carnality. Show
him/her that those things which are born of the flesh remain
flesh, but those things that are born of the spirit are spirit.[9]
Give him/her the understanding that to be carnally minded
is death but to be spiritually minded is life and peace.[10]

Flesh and blood cannot inherit your kingdom,
Father,[11] but the spiritual man receives all things. I pray
that you will so work in the life of my son/daughter that
he/she will ever strive to be a truly spiritual individual, one
who is truly led by your Spirit.[12] I pray that his/her desire
will ever be to seek those things which are above, where
Christ sits at your right hand, Father.[13]

Show my son/daughter that while bodily exercise is
profitable, godliness is profitable in every way.[14] Teach
him/her to pray,[15] to love you with all his/her heart,[16] to be
a witness to others[17] and to lead a life that is well-pleasing
in your sight, O Lord.[18]

References: (1) 1 Corinthians 2:14; (2) Matthew 22:37; (3) Deuteronomy
8:3; (4) Psalms 36:9; (5) Psalms 119:105; (6) John 16:13;
(7) Psalms 51:10; (8) Matthew 6:33; (9) John 3:6; (10) Romans
8:6; (11) 1 Corinthians 15:50; (12) Romans 8:14; (13) Colossians
3:1; (14) 1 Timothy 4:8; (15) Luke 11:1; (16) Matthew 22:37;
(17) Acts 1:8; (18) Hebrews 13:21.

Spiritual Nurture

Key Thought: "All growth that is not towards God is growing to decay" (George MacDonald).

Key Scripture: *"And, ye fathers, provoke not your children to wrath: but bring them up in the nurture and admonition of the Lord" (Eph. 6:4).*

Prayer: Dear Lord, I come to you now in behalf of my child, _____, who will need your spiritual nurture and admonition throughout his/her life. Help me to lay a foundation for him/her that will enable him/her to build his/her life on the solid Rock of Jesus Christ and your Word.[1] Help him/her to grow in knowledge, stature and in favor with you and others.[2]

As a newborn babe, help my child to desire the sincere milk of your Word that he/she may grow thereby.[3] Help him/her to realize that hiding your Word in his/her heart will keep him/her from sin.[4] Lord, lead him/her to memorize and meditate upon your Word so that he/she will not sin against you.[5]

Keep my son/daughter in the hollow of your hand,[6] so that he/she will not be tossed to and fro with every wind of doctrine. Instead, Lord God above, I pray that my child will learn to speak the truth in love, growing up into the Lord Jesus Christ in all things.[7]

Bring godly teachers, pastors and youth leaders into his/her life that will be able to fortify the work you are doing in his/her life at all times so that my son/daughter will be able to grow in grace and in the knowledge of our Lord and Savior Jesus Christ. To Him be glory both now and forever.[8]

Father, I pray that my child's faith will grow exceedingly and that his/her love will always abound.[9] Teach him/her to reverently fear your name so that the Sun of righteousness will arise in his/her life with healing in His wings.[10]

Create in _____ a pure heart, O God, and renew a steadfast spirit within him/her.[11] Fill him/her with your Spirit.[12] Impart the joy of your salvation and grant him/her a willing spirit to sustain him/her.[13] Thank you for the mighty promises of your Word, dear Lord.

References: *(1) Matthew 16:18; (2) Luke 2:52; (3) 1 Peter 2:2; (4) Psalms 119:9; (5) Psalms 119:11; (6) Isaiah 40:12; (7) Ephesians 4:15; (8) 2 Peter 3:18; (9) 2 Thessalonians 1:3; (10) Malachi 4:2; (11) Psalms 51:10, NIV; (12) Acts 2:38-39; (13) Psalms 51:12, NIV.*

Strength and Vitality

Key Thought: The power of God is the true source of strength.

Key Scripture: *"O Lord our Lord, how excellent is thy name in all the earth! who hast set thy glory above the heavens. Out of the mouth of babes and sucklings hast thou ordained strength because of thine enemies, that thou mightest still the enemy and the avenger" (Ps. 8:1-2).*

Prayer: O Lord, you are our strength[1] and in you there is abundant life and provision.[2] You are a strong tower,[3] and you are life itself.[4] I pray, Father, that you will reveal these truths about your strength to my son/daughter, _____, and grant that he/she would be strengthened with might by your Spirit.[5]

Teach _____ to seek you and your strength continually from his/her early years and throughout adulthood. May he/she ever seek your face, O Lord.[6] Show my son/daughter that the joy you impart is our source of strength.[7]

I will love you, O Lord, my strength. Reveal to my child that you are his/her rock, fortress and deliverer. Let him/her ever trust in you as his/her strength, and remind him/her to call upon you in the day of trouble.[8] Let my son/daughter know, O Lord, that you are his/her light and salvation, and because this is true, there is no need for him/her ever to fear. You are the strength of his/her life.[9]

Lord God, you are our salvation and our glory. You are the rock of our strength and our refuge. Teach my son/daughter that you are his/her refuge and strength — that his/her safe place is in you.[10] How I thank you, Father, that your grace will always be sufficient for my son/daughter. Show him/her that your strength will be made perfect in his/her time of weakness. Let the power of your Son, Jesus Christ, always rest upon him/her[11] and make him/her strong in you, Lord, and in the power of your might.[12]

References: (1) Psalms 27:1; (2) John 10:10; (3) Psalms 61:3; (4) John 1:4; (5) Ephesians 3:16; (6) 1 Chronicles 16:11; (7) Nehemiah 8:10; (8) Psalms 18:1; (9) Psalms 27:1; (10) Psalms 62:7; (11) 2 Corinthians 12:9; (12) Ephesians 6:10.

A Student

Key Thought: "The greatest good is wisdom" (Augustine).

Key Scripture: *"Study to shew thyself approved unto God, a workman that needeth not to be ashamed, rightly dividing the word of truth" (2 Tim. 2:15).*

Prayer: Father, I pray for _____ who is facing all the challenges and difficulties of school responsibilities. Impart your wisdom to him/her so that he/she will understand that wisdom in the principal thing.[1] Motivate him/her to seek wisdom and to gain understanding.[2]

Grace and mercy come from you, Lord.[3] As you did for Daniel and the three Hebrew children, I ask that you give my child(ren) knowledge and skill in all learning and wisdom that he/she/they may be excellent in all his/her/their schoolwork and activities.[4]

You are a very present help to _____ _____ in all areas of his/her life.[5] Help him/her to call upon you when the demands of scholastic life threaten to overwhelm him/her.

May _____ realize that you have a plan and purpose for his/her life.[6] Give him/her the motivation to pursue your goals for him/her. Protect him/her from all harmful influences.

Keep his/her mind stayed on you.[7] When philosophies and theories of this world oppose his/her faith, help him/her to maintain a constant focus on you, to run his/her course with patience, looking unto you, Lord Jesus, the author and finisher of his/her faith.[8]

May I always be faithful with my responsibilities to _____ , to pray for him/her, to look for ways to encourage him/her, to listen to him/her and to provide helpful counsel to him/her. Help me to be a true friend to him/her, one who loves at all times and never gives up.[9]

Bless _____ with clarity of mind as he/she studies. Help him/her to be diligent and to avoid the error of procrastination concerning assignments. Remind him/her to remain faithful even in the things he or she may consider unimportant.[10]

Give him/her faith in your promise, as he/she faces tests and exams, that by your great Comforter, the Holy Spirit, you will bring all things to his/her remembrance.[11]

Thank you for providing us with all we need to meet the challenges of life. You have equipped _____ _____ with the necessary abilities to do well in school. Help _____ to remember to be thankful to you for the abilities and aptitude you have given to him/her.[12]

Although it is sometimes true that much study is a weariness of the flesh,[13] I pray for _____ , that you will renew his/her strength.[14] May his/her greatest desire always be to follow in your steps, O Lord.[15] Bless him/her and use him/her to bring glory to your name.

References: *(1) Proverbs 4:7; (2) Proverbs 4:5; (3) 1 Timothy 1:2; (4) Daniel 1:17, 5:14; (5) Psalms 46:1; (6) Jeremiah 29:11; (7) Isaiah 26:3; (8) Hebrews 12:2; (9) Proverbs 17:17; (10) Luke 16:10; (11) John 14:26; (12) Ephesians 5:20; (13) Ecclesiastes 12:12; (14) Isaiah 40:31; (15) 1 Peter 2:21.*

Success

Key Thought: "Success is from above" (Sir Henry Lansdowne).

Key Scripture: *"This book of the law shall not depart out of thy mouth; but thou shalt meditate therein day and night, that thou mayest observe to do according to all that is written therein: for then thou shalt make thy way prosperous, and then thou shalt have good success" (Josh. 1:8).*

Prayer: Father, your Word shows us the way to success. Thank you for the multitude of promises contained in your Word. I come to you now asking for success for my son/daughter, _____. May he/she realize early on that the key to success, happiness and prosperity is found in knowing Jesus Christ as Lord and meditating upon your Word.[1]

Let the delight of my son/daughter be in your law, O Lord, and in your law may he/she meditate both day and night.[2] In this way I know that he/she will become like a tree planted by the rivers of water, that brings forth fruit in the proper season and whatsoever he/she does will prosper.[3] Praise your mighty name.

Those who love you, Lord, will prosper in all that they do.[4] Peace will be within the walls of their home and prosperity will fill their dwelling place.[5] This is my prayer for _____, that he/she would love you with all his/her heart, soul, mind and strength,[6] always realizing that you love him/her with an everlasting love.[7]

I wish and pray, above all else, for my son/daughter that he/she would know you personally, receive the gift of eternal life,[8] and prosper and be in health throughout his/her life.[9]

Show my son/daughter the vital importance of keeping the words of your covenant with him/her so that he/she will do your bidding and thereby enjoy success in all that he/she does.[10] Bless him/her with your loving presence[11] and guide him/her watchfully with your eye,[12] for your eyes upon the righteous and your ears are open to their cry.[13] Thank you, Lord.

References: *(1) Joshua 1:8; (2) Psalms 1:2; (3) Psalms 1:3; (4) Psalms 122:6; (5) Psalms 122:7; (6) Matthew 22:37; (7) Psalms 100:5; (8) Romans 6:23; (9) 3 John 2; (10) Psalms 132:12; (11) Psalms 34:18; (12) Psalms 32:8; (13) Psalms 34:15.*

Talents and Abilities

Key Thought: Our abilities are gifts from God.

Key Scripture: *"And I have filled him with the Spirit of God, with skill, ability and knowledge in all kinds of crafts" (Exod. 31:3, NIV).*

Prayer: Lord God, I pray for my son/daughter, _____
_____, that you will guide him/her to know that nothing is impossible with you.[1] Indeed, all things are possible to those who believe.[2] I pray that my son/daughter will always be a believer in your miracle-working power.

Help _____ to realize that without you he/she can do nothing.[3] Through you, however, he/she can accomplish all things.[4] Keep him/her ever conscious of the reality that you, Lord, are the potter; he/she is the clay,[5] and that you are molding and shaping him/her into the image of your Son.[6] I thank you for your continuing workmanship in his/her life.[7]

My son/daughter came into this world with sealed orders from your hand, O Lord. I ask you to help him/her to discover his/her calling and to recognize always that his/her sufficiency is of you.[8] May he/she never neglect the gift that is in him/her.[9] I pray that _____

_____ will allow you to guide him/her into all that you have for him/her.

You are the Giver of every good and perfect gift, Father.[10] I desire for my son/daughter to recognize this truth early in his/her life and to respond with thanksgiving. Help him/her to be able to give thanks in everything, to pray without ceasing and to rejoice evermore,[11] both for who you are and all you are doing in his/her life.

Teach him/her your way in all things, Father.[12] Reveal your will to him/her. Help him/her to say yes to every command you present, to delight to do your will[13] and to recognize that his/her talents are gifts from you to be used to bring glory to your name. May he/she never waste or ignore the talents you present to him/her.[14] Let him/her ever realize that all things are of you, Father.[15]

I thank you for the gifts and abilities you have given to _____. Help me to encourage him/her to discover these talents and to put them to good use in building your Kingdom on earth.

References: *(1) Matthew 17:20; (2) Mark 9:23; (3) John 15:5; (4) Philippians 4:13; (5) Isaiah 64:8; (6) Romans 8:29; (7) Ephesians 2:10; (8) 2 Corinthians 3:5; (9) 1 Timothy 4:14; (10) James 1:17; (11) 1 Thessalonians 5:16-18; (12) Psalms 18:30; (13) Psalms 40:8; (14) Matthew 25:14-29; (15) Colossians 1:16.*

To Have a Child

Key Thought: God hears your prayers.

Key Scripture: *"Now unto him that is able to do exceeding abundantly above all that we ask or think, according to the power that worketh in us, Unto him be glory in the church by Christ Jesus throughout all ages, world without end. Amen" (Eph. 3:20-21).*

Prayer: Heavenly Father, the One in whom we live and move and have our being,[1] I praise you and thank you for the precious gift of children. They make life both sweet and challenging. I come to you with thanksgiving and faith, and I ask you to bless me with a baby whom I can raise in your nurture and admonition.[2] I realize that children are an heritage from you, and the fruit of the womb is a reward that you give to your people.[3]

You make the barren woman to be a joyful mother as you did in the case of Sara[4] and of Hannah.[5] It was through faith that Sara received strength to conceive seed, and she was delivered of a child when she was past age because she trusted in your faithfulness, Lord.[6]

Help me to keep on believing and to trust you totally in this matter of desiring a child. Lord, may your will be done.[7] Impart faith and hope to my heart to keep me from all discouragement. Protect my heart and mind so that I will never be confounded or disheartened by the negative words of others.[8]

As arrows are in the hand of a mighty man, so are children of the youth. Happy is the man that has his quiver full of them, and they shall not be ashamed for they will speak with the enemies in the gate.[9] I claim this promise from you, Father.

Thank you for every prayer promise from your Word. You have assured me that whatsoever I ask I will receive from you if I keep your commandments and do those things that are pleasing in your sight.[10]

Thank you, Father, for hearing my prayer. I know that if I will pray in accordance with your will as it is revealed in your Word, I can have confidence that you are hearing me and that you will answer my prayer.[11] I do have confidence in you, Father, and I thank you for your promise that declares you will give me the desires of my heart.[12] Having a child, Lord, is my heart's greatest desire at this time, and I ask you to bless me with a baby and with the wisdom I need to be a good parent under your Lordship.

References: *(1) Acts 17:28; (2) Ephesians 6:4; (3) Psalms 127:3; (4) Psalms 113:9; (5) 1 Samuel 1:20;2:1-2; (6) Hebrews 11:11; (7) Luke 11:2; (8) Psalms 22:4-5; (9) Psalms 127:4-5; (10) 1 John 3:22-23; (11) 1 John 5:14; (12) Psalms 37:4.*

A Troubled Youth

Key Thought: Each boy and girl has a set of sealed orders.

Key Scripture: *"Wherewithal shall a young man cleanse his way? by taking heed thereto according to thy word. With my whole heart have I sought thee: O let me not wander from thy commandments. Thy word have I hid in mine heart, that I might not sin against thee" (Ps. 119:9-11).*

Prayer: Heavenly Father, move in the life of _____ _____, my son/daughter who seems to be troubled at this point in his/her life. I pray that he/she will search for you with all his/her heart. Remind him/her of the need to follow your commandments,[1] and to obey his/her parents.[2] Shield and protect him/her from the evil one.[3] Let all strategies and schemes of the enemy against his/her life be canceled, now in the name of Jesus.[4]

Convict _____ of his/her need for you. Draw him/her to abundant life in you.[5] I thank you that you do have a plan and a purpose for his/her life.[6]

May _____ become like the Prodigal Son who realized in his heart that he needed to return to his father.[7] May _____ return (either physically or spiritually) to our family and to you, O Father.

Turn _____'s heart toward you and toward me, Lord, and help me to keep my heart right toward him/her.[8] We are living in difficult times of disobedience and rebellion, but you, Lord, are more powerful than all the influences of Satan. Turn any disobedience in _____'s life to the wisdom of the just. I thank you that you are making ready a people who are prepared for you.[9]

Help _____ to remember you in the days of his/her youth, while the evil days come not nor the years draw nigh.[10] Keep him/her from all potentially harmful influences of his/her peer group.

My Father, I recognize you as the guide of our youths.[11] I pray for young people in general, and for my son/daughter, _____, in particular, that they would find you early and be set free from the prevailing philosophies and behaviors of our day. Accompany _____ with restlessness until he/she finds his/her rest in you.

References: *(1) Psalms 119:9; (2) Ephesians 6:1; (3) Matthew 6:13; (4) Ephesians 6:11; (5) John 10:10; (6) Jeremiah 29:11; (7) Luke 15:11-32; (8) Malachi 4:5-6; (9) Luke 1:16-17; (10) Ecclesiastes 12:1; (11) Jeremiah 3:4.*

Truth and Honesty

Key Thought: "Truth makes the devil blush" (Thomas Fuller).

Key Scripture: *"And of his fulness have all we received, and grace for grace. For the law was given by Moses, but grace and truth came by Jesus Christ" (John 1:16-17).*

Prayer: Lord God of the universe, I come to you in behalf of my son/daughter, _____. Bless him/her, Lord, with a love for truth and honesty at all times. I thank you that your Word is truth,[1] and I ask that you would give _____ a hunger for your Word that would lead him/her to always walk in truth and honesty.[2]

Though heaven and earth will pass away, your words will never pass away.[3] Thank you, Father, for this promise and for all the promises of your sacred Word. Help my son/daughter to love the truth and peace at all times.[4]

Your counsels of old, Father, are faithfulness and truth.[5] Guide my son/daughter throughout his/her life. It is so wonderful to know that everyone that is of the truth hears your voice.[6] May _____ ever be one who hears your voice. I thank you that your sheep know your voice and you know your sheep.[7] Keep _____ secure at all times in your fold, O Lord, our Shepherd, the Good Shepherd.[8]

I ask that you would lead my son/daughter to buy the truth and never sell it at any price.[9] May he/she always speak the truth in love,[10] giving priority at all times to speaking what you speak to him/her.[11]

Thank you, Father, for the certainty that your truth will endure throughout all generations.[12] Your Son, our Lord and Savior Jesus Christ, is the way, the truth and the life,[13] and the works of His hands are verity, truth and judgment. All His commandments are sure.[14] I pray for
_____ , Lord, that he/she would early and always know your truth, and I pray that the truth would set him/her free.[15]

I ask you to guide my son/daughter to come to your light, O Lord, so that his/her deeds would be made manifest,[16] and that he would always want to walk in truth and honesty. Sanctify him/her through your truth.[17] I rejoice in the certain knowledge that the truth is in Jesus,[18] and, Lord, I ask that you will keep my son/daughter from all lies and deception as he/she learns to walk in the footsteps of Jesus who cannot lie. Like your apostle, John, I have no greater joy, Father, than to know my child walks in the truth.[19]

References: *(1) John 17:17; (2) 3 John 4; (3) Matthew 24:35; (4) Zechariah 8:19; (5) Isaiah 25:1; (6) John 18:37; (7) John 10:27; (8) Psalms 23:1; (9) Proverbs 23:23; (10) Ephesians 4:15; (11) John 18:37; (12) Psalms 100:5; (13) John 14:6; (14) Psalms 111:7; (15) John 8:32; (16) John 3:21; (17) John 17:17; (18) Ephesians 4:21; (19) 3 John 4.*

An Unborn Child

Key Thought: Every child is a precious gift.

Key Scripture: *"For thou hast possessed my reins: thou hast covered me in my mother's womb. I will praise thee; for I am fearfully and wonderfully made: marvelous are thy works; and that my soul knoweth right well" (Ps. 139:13-14).*

Prayer: Thank you, Father, for the precious gift of life, for this tiny person you are creating. To have the honor of welcoming this new baby into our home and family is a joyous privilege indeed. I praise you, Father, for this child you are giving to us. He/she is fearfully and wonderfully made.[1]

Cover the womb with your love.[2] Bless this child with a supernatural awareness of your presence.[3] May he/she always know that you are with him/her [4] and experience fullness of joy.[5] May he/she always be sensitive to your Spirit, Lord, and walk in your truth.[6] As he/she learns to bond together with us/me, his/her parent(s), may he/she also learn to bond with you, Father.[7]

I thank you, Lord, that you see my/our baby's substance even as he/she is being made in secret.[8] You know him/her intimately. Begin even now, Lord, to call him/her and to prepare his/her heart to respond to you.[9]

Grant health, strength and vitality to this precious child as you form him/her in the womb.[10]

I pray that the birthing process will go smoothly,[11] and be safe[12] and peaceful.[13] As you bring him/her forth from the womb, I pray that you will make him/her to trust in you.[14] May he/she be cast upon you from the womb, and know you as his/her God.[15]

Strengthen this child even now, Father. May he/she learn to trust you with all his/her heart. Guide him/her from the womb.[16] Fashion him/her according to your purposes.[17] Form him/her from the womb to be your servant, Father.[18]

Lord Jesus, I thank you for your great love for children.[19] My heart rejoices in your goodness, and I bask in your blessings and in your salvation.[20] I dedicate the life and future of this unborn child to you and your service.

References: (1) Psalms 139:14; (2) Psalms 139:13; (3) Luke 1:41; (4) Psalms 139:7; (5) Psalms 16:11; (6) John 16:13; (7) 2 Corinthians 6:16; (8) Psalms 139:15; (9) Isaiah 49:1; (10) Isaiah 44:2, NIV; (11) 1 Timothy 2:15; (12) Psalms 4:8; (13) Psalms 29:11; (14) Psalms 22:9, NIV; (15) Psalms 22:10, nivNIV; (16) Psalms 71:6, NIV; (17) Job 31:15; (18) Isaiah 49:5; (19) Matthew 19:14; (20) 1 Samuel 2:1.

A Vocation

Key Thought: "He who labors as he prays lifts his heart to God with his hands" (Bernard of Clairvaux).

Key Scripture: *"And that ye study to be quiet, and to do your own business, and to work with your own hands, as we commanded you: That ye may walk honestly toward them that are without, and that ye may have lack of nothing" (1 Thess. 4:11-12).*

Prayer: Lord God, I come to you now in behalf of my son/daughter, _____, asking you to lead him/her into the career that is perfectly in line with your will for him/her. I pray, Father, that you will always provide him/her with work to do, so that he/she will feel productive, worthwhile and will never have to owe others anything except love.[1]

Strengthen and prepare _____ for the work you are calling him/her to do. May his/her hands never be weak. Give him/her the realization that you have a special job — a calling — for him/her to perform and help him/her to realize that his/her work will always be rewarded by you.[2]

Give him/her the grace to count it all joy during the times when things don't work out as he/she hopes, realizing that the trying of his/her faith will work patience into his/her life. Let patience have its perfect work in his/her life so that he/she will be perfect and entire, wanting nothing.[3]

I pray that you will bless _____ with the gift of faith. May he/she always know that his/her faith is counted as righteousness in your sight.[4] Good things always stem from faith in you and your Son, Father. You are the Giver of every good and perfect gift (including employment), the Father of lights, with whom there is no variableness nor shadow of turning.[5] Enlighten the life of my son/daughter with a knowledge of your will for his/her life.

Father, your Word says that where there is no vision the people perish.[6] Give your vision and direction so that he/she can set the proper goals for his/her life in the realms of education, vocation, family and ministry.[7] You, Lord, have the power to put down the mighty from their seats, and the power to exalt those of low degree.[8] Prepare a place of employment for _____ even now that will enable him/her to utilize all the special gifts and talents you have given to him/her.

References: *(1) Romans 13:8; (2) 2 Chronicles 15:7; (3) James 1:1-4; (4) Galatians 3:6; (5) James 1:17; (6) Proverbs 29:18; (7) John 16:13; (8) Luke 1:52.*

Walking in Contentment

Key Thought: "A contented mind is the greatest blessing...in this world" (Joseph Addison).

Key Scripture: *"But godliness with contentment is great gain. For we brought nothing into this world, and it is certain we can carry nothing out. And having food and raiment let us be therewith content" (1 Tim. 6:6-8).*

Prayer: Teach me the meaning of true contentment, Lord, so that I can model its blessings of peace and joy in front of my son/daughter, _____.
I pray that throughout his/her life, that he/she will learn to be content in whatsoever state he/she finds himself/herself[1] and to be free from inner restlessness that would drive him/her to search for contentment in worldly pleasures.[2] Reveal to him/her that true rest and contentment come by way of faith in you, Lord, and by obedience to your Word.[3] Let him/her know how to be abased and how to abound, how to walk close to you and trust you both in the hard times and in the good times.[4] It is the prayer of my heart that _____ will find and keep the contentment that comes to everyone who realizes that they can endure and face anything through Jesus Christ who strengthens us.[5]

Give _____ the wonderful knowledge that you are with him/her, and in so doing, I pray that he/she will find true contentment of spirit,[6] peace of heart and mind,[7] and the rest that comes from you.[8] Feed him/her with food that is convenient for him/her, and may he/she be satisfied with all that you provide for him/her.[9] Impart to my child your glorious peace that passes all understanding.[10]

Take away any and all covetousness or envy from the heart of my son/daughter, Lord.[11] Give him/her the understanding that material riches do not bring happiness.[12] Teach him/her to trust you[13] to meet his/her every need,[14] to find full contentment in the realization that you will never leave nor forsake him/her.[15]

Help him/her to thankfully enjoy the material blessings you give to him/her.[16] Give him/her wisdom to handle those blessings well[17] and to always cheerfully receive from you, give to your kingdom and share with others.[18] You, Lord, will bless him/her as he/she does these things, and I know that this will bring him/her special inner contentment.[19]

Enable _____ to ever know that you are his/her helper, and because this is true, he/she never has to fear.[20] I pray that he/she will always believe and know that your people will never hunger or thirst,[21] that you never forsake the righteous,[22] and that his/her cup will always overflow with the blessings you provide.[23]

Give abundant life to my son/daughter.[24] Reveal yourself to him/her as the God of more than enough, the One who is ever able and willing to do exceeding abundantly beyond all that he/she can ask or think.[25] May your contentment, Lord, which is found through godliness, fill his/her heart even now, and forever.[26]

References: *(1) Philippians 4:11; (2) Titus 2:12; (3) Hebrews 4; (4) Philippians 4:12; (5) Philippians 4:13; (6) Hebrews 13:5; (7) Colossians 3:15; (8) Hebrews 4:1; (9) Proverbs 30:8; (10) Philippians 4:7; (11) Hebrews 13:5; (12) Romans 14:17; (13) Proverbs 3:5-6; (14) Philippians 4:19; (15) Hebrews 13:5; (16) 1 Timothy 6:8; (17) James 1:5; (18) Matthew 10:8; (19) John 13:17; (20) Hebrews 13:6; (21) Revelation 7:16; (22) Psalms 37:25; (23) Psalms 23:5; (24) John 10:10; (25) Ephesians 3:20; (26) 1 Timothy 6:6-8.*

Walking in Faith

Key Thought: "Faith is not a sense, nor sight, nor reason, but taking God at His Word" (Arthur Benoni Evans).

Key Scripture: *"Now faith is the substance of things hoped for, the evidence of things not seen....But without faith it is impossible to please him: for he that cometh to God must believe that he is, and that he is a rewarder of them that diligently seek him" (Heb. 11:1,6).*

Prayer: Eternal Father, grant unto my son/daughter, _____ , a desire to walk in faith through your Word.[1.] Impart to his/her heart the realization that all things are possible to a person who truly believes.[2] Help him/her to add to his/her faith goodness, and to his/her goodness, to add knowledge. To his/her knowledge, I pray that he/she would add self-control, then perseverance, godliness, brotherly kindness and love.[3]

Reveal to my son/daughter that whatsoever is not of faith is sin.[4] Lead him/her to understand that your Word unlocks the doors of faith for him/her to enter. Let him/her know that walking in faith is the most exciting life-style of all.

When doubt threatens my child's faith, Father, I pray that you would increase his/her faith.[5] Strengthen him/her to cast all doubt away in the full knowledge that doubt

exalts itself against you, Lord.[6] Keep my son/daughter
from double-mindedness;[7] may he/she always be single-
minded, persevering in faith, looking unto the Lord Jesus
Christ who is the Author and Finisher of his/her faith.[8]

Show _____ that the just shall
live by faith — your faith, O Lord.[9] Give him/her faith to
move the mountains in his/her life as you guide and direct
him/her. Because I know that nothing is impossible to a
person who walks in the faith you give,[10] I pray that you
will fill his/her heart with the faith he/she needs to overcome the problems in his/her life.

May _____ be a person who
reads the Bible, thinking and meditating upon your Word
both day and night,[11] thereby receiving the faith, insight
and wisdom that your Word provides.[12]

I ask that my son/daughter would become like
Stephen — a man who was full of your grace, faith and
power, and did great things in your name, O Lord.[13] May
_____ ever continue in your faith,
grounded and settled, and never moved away from the
hope your gospel provides.[14] Thank you, Father, for the
grace and the faith you are imparting to his/her heart.[15]

References: (1) Romans 10:17; (2) Mark 9:23; (3) 2 Peter 1:5-7,
NIV; (4) Romans 14:22-23; (5) Luke 17:5; (6) 2 Corinthians
10:5; (7) James 1:6-8; (8) Hebrews 12:2; (9) Habakkuk 2:4;
(10) Matthew 17:20; (11) Psalms 1:2; (12) Proverbs 2:6; (13) Acts
6:8; (14) Colossians 1:23; (15) Ephesians 2:8-9.

Walking in Faithfulness

Key Thought: When we are full of faith we will be faithful.

Key Thought: *"His lord said unto him, Well done, good and faithful servant; thou hast been faithful over a few things, I will make thee ruler over many things: enter thou into the joy of thy lord"* (Matt. 25:23).

Prayer: Great is your faithfulness, O God, my Father.[1] Through your Spirit, my son/daughter, _____
_____, can acquire faithfulness for his/her life. This is my prayer for him/her, Father, that he/she would learn to let this fruit of your Spirit grow and be faithful in the little things as well as the bigger things of life. Help him/her to see, Lord, that as he/she is faithful in the small things, you can entrust the weightier things of the Kingdom unto him/her.[2]

Show my son/daughter that faithfulness stems from faith and involves steadiness, consistency and stability,[3] and reveal to him/her that these qualities will come only as he/she learns to keep his/her priorities in order. Let him/her see how truly important faithfulness is to you, Father.[4]

Lead and strengthen my son/daughter always to be faithful to you, to others, to his/her personal responsibilities and to his/her values so that others will know they can depend on him/her.[5]

Help me always to set an example of faithfulness before my son/daughter. May he/she always know me as a promise-keeper, Lord. Thank you for the fruit of faithfulness in my life, Lord.[6] I ask you to be faithful through me so that my son/daughter would want to cultivate that same fruit in his/her life from this moment forward.

Teach my son/daughter to be a good steward over all that you entrust into his/her care.[7] Keep him/her from the error of seeing possessions, talents or anything else as his/her personal possessions, and reveal to him/her that everything in the universe belongs to you.[8] Through his/her faithfulness, Father, I pray that others will always recognize my son/daughter to be trustworthy and dependable.

References: *(1) Lamentations 3:23; (2) Luke 19:17; (3) 2 Thessalonians 3:3; (4) Proverbs 28:20; (5) Proverbs 13:17; (6) Galatians 5:22; (7) Luke 12:37; (8) Psalms 24:1.*

Walking in Gentleness

Key Thought: Gentleness is a kind disposition toward others.

Key Scripture: *"Thou hast also given me the shield of thy salvation; and thy right hand hath holden me up, and thy gentleness hath made me great" (Ps. 18:35).*

Prayer: Gentle and gracious Lord, sometimes it seems that the beautiful quality of gentleness is a forgotten trait in our present age. Like meekness and self-control, it is a fruit of your Holy Spirit in our lives,[1] and I thank you that you want to develop the quality of gentleness in the life of my son/daughter, _____.

Teach him/her to be truly gentle, Father, in all the relationships and responsibilities of his/her life, even with those who oppose you and him/her.[2] Keep _____ _____ from all rudeness in each relationship and acquaintanceship, even with those who disappoint him/her.[3]

Help _____ to remember, Lord, that a meek and quiet spirit is of great value to you. Adorn the hidden man of his/her heart with your gentleness which is not corruptible.[4]

May my son/daughter never confuse gentleness with weakness, but to see it as it truly is, a source of genuine spiritual strength. Thank you, Father, for giving us so many examples of the strength of gentleness in your Word. I pray that _____ will be able to identify with the lives of David, Jacob, Stephen, John and Paul who showed forth your gentleness in a variety of ways.[5]

Thank you, Father, for the gentle spirit of our Lord and Savior, Jesus Christ, who constantly exhibited your kindness, meekness and strength.[6] Impart these qualities to the spirit of my son/daughter, Lord, and may he/she reflect your gentleness in all his/her ways.

Help him/her to be kind and gentle to others, tenderhearted and forgiving of others, even as you, Father, for Christ's sake have forgiven him/her.[7]

Fill _____ with your Spirit, Lord, so that he/she will produce the fruit of gentleness in all of his/her relationships and responsibilities.[8]

References: (1) Galatians 5:22; (2) 2 Timothy 2:24; (3) Titus 3:2; (4) 1 Peter 3:4; (5) 2 Corinthians 6:1-10; (6) 2 Corinthians 10:1; (7) Ephesians 4:32; (8) Galatians 5:22.

Walking in God's Fullness

Key Thought: Our God is awesome.

Key Scripture: *"Wherefore, my beloved, as you have always obeyed, not as in my presence only, but now much more in my absence, work out your own salvation with fear and trembling" (Phil. 2:12).*

Prayer: I bow my knees to you, God, the Father of my/our Lord Jesus Christ, of whom the whole family in heaven and earth is named, that you would grant my child, _____ , according to the riches of your glory, to be strengthened with might by your Spirit in the inner man (person, being), that Christ may dwell in his/her heart by faith; and that he/she, being rooted and grounded in love, may be able to comprehend with all saints what is the breadth, and length, and depth and height; and to know (and experience) the love of Christ, which passes knowledge, that he/she may be filled with all of your fullness.

Now unto you who are able to do exceedingly abundantly above all that we ask or think, according to your power that works within us, unto you, O God, be glory in the Church by Christ Jesus throughout all ages, world without end. Amen.[1]

References: (1) Ephesians 3:14-21.

Walking in God's Word

Key Thought: "Nobody ever outgrows Scripture; the Book widens and deepens with our years" (Charles Haddon Spurgeon).

Key Scripture: *"This book of the law shall not depart out of thy mouth; but thou shalt meditate therein day and night, that thou mayest observe to do according to all that is written therein: for then thou shalt make thy way prosperous, and then thou shalt have good success" (Josh. 1:8).*

Prayer: Heavenly Father, the Father of our Lord and Savior Jesus Christ, as I come to you now in behalf of my son/daughter, I ask that you would grant to him/her, out of the riches of your glory, that he/she would be strengthened with might by your Spirit in his/her inner man.[1] Help him/her to be rooted and grounded in your Word, O Lord, to be like the noble Bereans who studied the Scriptures daily.[2]

Reveal to my son/daughter his/her great need to study well so that he/she would be approved of you, a workman who never needs to be ashamed, because he/she is rightly dividing your Word of truth.[3] Lord, I ask you now to show my son/daughter that your Word is a lamp unto his/her feet and a light unto his/her path.[4]

Let _____ see the power of your Word, Lord, that it is like a two-edged sword that is able to divide between soul and spirit and it is a discerner of the thoughts and intentions of the human heart.[5] Let him/her know your Word as the sword of your Spirit, the weapon he/she can use to defeat the enemy in his/her life.[6] Let him/her see that your Word is like a mighty hammer that is ever able to break the enemy's yoke, and it is a fire that burns away the chaff of life.[7]

When others attempt to distract my son/daughter from the truths of your Word, help him/her always to remember that your Word is true, that it is a shield, a mighty buckler to all those who trust in you.[8] Help him/her to remember that it is by taking heed to your Word that one is able to cleanse his way; lead my son/daughter to hide your Word in his/her heart so that he/she will not sin against you.[9]

References: *(1) Ephesians 3:16; (2) Acts 17:11; (3) 2 Timothy 2:15; (4) Psalms 119:105; (5) Hebrews 4:12; (6) Ephesians 6:17; (7) Jeremiah 23:29; (8) Psalms 91:4; (9) Psalms 119:9-11.*

Walking in Goodness

Key Thought: The word "goodness" comes from the word "God," just as true goodness comes from God himself.

Key Scripture: *"Surely goodness and mercy shall follow me all the days of my life: and I will dwell in the house of the Lord for ever" (Ps. 23:6).*

Prayer: Heavenly Father, you are the Author of all goodness. I pray that my son/daughter, _____ _____, will taste and see that you are good.[1] You are merciful and gracious, longsuffering, and abundant in goodness and truth.[2] I pray that my son/daughter will bear the fruit of goodness in his/her life bountifully, abundantly, and constantly.[3]

Reveal to _____ that you are the one true God, and that your words are true. You have promised goodness to your servants, Lord.[4] Assure _____ _____ that your goodness and mercy will follow him/her all the days of his/her life as long as he/she puts you first.[5] Help him/her to see, Lord, that any goodness he/she possesses stems directly from his/her relationship with you.[6] You alone are good, Lord.[7]

I pray that _____ will rejoice in your goodness,[8] that he/she will choose to be glad and merry in heart because of the goodness you have shown to him/her.[9] Give him/her the faith to see your goodness in the land of the living.[10] Reveal to him/her that you have laid up your goodness for all those who fear you.[11] Your goodness, O Lord, endures continually,[12] and I praise you that you are filling _____ with your goodness even now. Satisfy his/her soul with your goodness, Lord.[13]

Thank you for your promise that you will supply goodness to all those who continue in your ways.[14] I pray that _____ will always walk in your goodness, desire to show forth your goodness to others, so that he/she would always be able to live godly and to admonish others in love.[15]

Fill _____ with goodness, and righteousness, and truth.[16]

References: *(1) Psalms 34:8; (2) Exodus 34:6; (3) Galatians 5:22; (4) 2 Samuel 7:28; (5) Psalms 23:6; (6) John 15:5; (7) Luke 18:19; (8) 2 Chronicles 6:41; (9) 2 Chronicles 7:10; (10) Psalms 27:13; (11) Psalms 31:19; (12) Psalms 52:1; (13) Psalms 107:9; (14) Romans 11:22; (15) Romans 15:14; (16) Ephesians 5:9.*

Walking in Joy

Key Thought: J-O-Y comes from Jesus, others and you.

Key Scripture: *"A merry heart maketh a cheerful countenance: but by sorrow of the heart the spirit is broken" (Prov. 15:13).*

Prayer: Dear Lord, it is your joy that gives people strength,[1] and I pray that you will impart your joy to my son/daughter, _____. It thrills me to know that you want him/her to experience your joy, and I ask you to introduce my son/daughter to your kingdom where he/she will find your righteousness, peace and joy in the Holy Spirit.[2] Give him/her joy unspeakable and full of glory as he/she reaches out to receive the end of his/her faith — the salvation of the soul.[3] Let the joy of his/her salvation keep him/her going at all times.

So fill _____ with your Spirit, Lord, that he/she will know the joy of your salvation.[4] May he/she ever rejoice in you, Father, because of your goodness and love and because of who you are.[5] May he/she finish the course of life with fullness of joy,[6] as he/she continues to look unto Jesus, the Author and Finisher of his/her faith.[7]

I pray that _____ will draw waters from your wells of salvation with joy.[8] Each day may he/she recognize that the new day was made by you, Lord; may the knowledge of your power and might lead him/her to rejoice and be glad in you.[9]

Show _____ that a merry heart makes for a cheerful countenance, Lord,[10] and I pray that others will be attracted to you by the joy that is reflected in his/her face. Clothe him/her with garments of salvation and cover him/her with a robe of righteousness.[11]

Fill _____ with your wisdom and spiritual understanding, Lord, that he/she might walk worthy of you unto all pleasing, being fruitful in every good work, and increasing in the knowledge of you; strengthened with all might, according to your glorious power, unto all patience and longsuffering with joyfulness;[12] giving thanks unto you, Father, always and in all things.[13]

References: *(1) Nehemiah 8:10; (2) Romans 14:17; (3) 1 Peter 1:8-9; (4) Psalms 51:12; (5) Psalms 5:11; (6) Acts 20:24; (7) Hebrews 12:2; (8) Isaiah 12:3; (9) Psalms 118:24; (10) Proverbs 15:13; (11) Isaiah 61:10; (12) Colossians 1:10-12; (13) Ephesians 5:20.*

Walking in the Light

Key Thought: There is no darkness in God.

Key Scripture: *"For you were once darkness, but now you are light in the Lord. Walk as children of light"* *(Eph. 5:8, NKJV).*

Prayer: Lord God, you have commanded us to walk in the light. Therefore, I pray for my child, _____ _____, that you would give him/her the desire to walk in the light of your Word[1] and the revelation of your Spirit.[2]

May your Word be a lamp unto his/her feet and a light unto his/her path.[3] Teach him/her to fulfill your desire for him/her to walk as one of your children in your light.[4]

May he/she be counted among those blessed ones who have learned to acclaim you and to walk in the light of your presence. May he/she rejoice in your name all day long and exalt in your righteousness.[5]

Thank you for saving my child and thereby making him/her able to be a partaker of the inheritance of the saints in light.[6]

Praise you, O Lord, for you have delivered us from the power of darkness and have translated us into the Kingdom

of the Son of your love, in whom we have redemption
through His blood, even the forgiveness of sins.[7]

*References: (1) Psalms 119:130; (2) Ephesians 1:17; (3) Psalms
119:105; (4) Ephesians 5:8; (5) Psalms 89:15-16; (6) Colossians
1:12; (7) Colossians 1:13-14.*

Walking in Love

Key Thought: God is love.

Key Scripture: *"There is no fear in love; but perfect love casteth out fear; because fear hath torment. He that feareth is not made perfect in love. We love him, because he first loved us"* (1 John 4:18-19).

Prayer: Father in heaven, thank you for loving the world so much that you gave your only begotten Son, that whosoever would believe in Him should not perish, but have everlasting life.[1] I pray that my son/daughter, _____ _____, would believe in Jesus Christ as his/her personal Savior and Lord.

May _____ always remember that the ability to love others and ourselves comes from your love.[2] I pray that he/she will learn that loving you leads to obedience; if we truly love you we will obey you.[3] Fill him/her with your perfect love that removes all fear.[4] Through your love, I pray that all people will recognize that _____ is your disciple, Lord.[5] May his/her love always be sincere, without any trace of hypocrisy.[6]

I thank you that there is no limit to your love, Father. It is from everlasting to everlasting. Shed your love abroad in the heart of my son/daughter[7] so that he/she will be able to comprehend with all saints the full extent of your love.[8]

Reveal to _____ that love's immediate response is always to give.[1] Because you are love, Father, it is possible for your love to flow through _____ to others. Help him/her to want to love, give and serve in the manner you demonstrated through Jesus Christ, our Lord.

I ask, Father, that the Lord Jesus would dwell in _____'s heart by faith. Root and ground him/her in your love. Above all else, Father, I ask that _____ would desire to know your love which passes knowledge, and may he/she be filled with all your fullness.[9]

Let him/her see that love is the most excellent way.[10] It has supremacy over every other gift. Teach _____ _____ to walk in love, to love others as you have loved him/her. Grant unto him/her an earnest desire to want to learn to love you, Father, with all his/her heart, soul, mind, and strength, and to love his/her neighbors as himself/herself.[11]

References: *(1) John 3:16; (2) 1 John 4:17-21; (3) John 14:15; (4) 1 John 4:18; (5) John 13:34,35; (6) Romans 12:9; (7) Romans 5:5; (8) Ephesians 3:18; (9) Ephesians 3:19; (10) 1 Corinthians 12:31; (11) Mark 12:30-31.*

Walking in Meekness

Key Thought: The meekness of the Lord is never weakness.

Key Scripture: *"Take my yoke upon you, and learn of me; for I am meek and lowly of heart: and ye shall find rest unto your souls" (Matt. 11:29)*

Prayer: Lord, I ask you to so move in the life of my son/daughter, _____, that he/she would want to take your yoke upon himself/herself and learn of you. Teach him/her the importance of genuine meekness of spirit. Let this fruit of your Spirit grow in his/her life daily.[1] I pray that _____ will choose to walk worthy of the calling to which you have called him/her.[2] I pray that he/she will walk with complete lowliness of mind (humility) and meekness, patience, and forbearance toward others, always seeking to make allowances for others through your love.[3]

Lead my son/daughter to put on the new man each day. I thank you, Father, that the new man is renewed in knowledge after your image.[4] Lead him/her to put on meekness, therefore, as the elect of your love, holy and beloved.[5] Help _____ to be slow to take offense at others and to patiently endure even when he/she is wrongfully persecuted.[6]

As your servant, Lord, help _____
_____. to learn not to strive, but to be apt to teach others in meekness, instructing those who oppose themselves, that they may be fully restored to you and your love.[7] Give _____the grace to lay aside all self-interest and to esteem others better and higher than himself/herself. Help him/her not to look just on his/her own things, but also on the things of others.[8]

Produce in _____'s life the quality of meekness that is pliable and teachable so that he/she may receive your Word with meekness, realizing that it is able to save his/her soul.[9]

Lord, I pray that _____ will commit to follow after righteousness, godliness, faith, love, patience and meekness throughout his/her life. Give him/her the constant strength to fight the good fight of faith and thereby to lay hold onto eternal life to which he/she has been called.[10]

References: (1) Galatians 5:23; (2) Ephesians 4:1; (3) Ephesians 4:2; (4) Colossians 3:10; (5) Colossians 3:12; (6) 1 Peter 2:20; (7) 2 Timothy 2:24-25; (8) Philippians 2:3-4; (9) James 1:21; (10) 1 Timothy 6:11-12.

Walking in Mercy and Humility

Key Thought: God's mercy endures forever.

Key Scripture: *"He hath shewed thee, O man, what is good; and what doth the Lord require of thee, but to do justly, and to love mercy, and to walk humbly with thy God?" (Mic. 6:8).*

Prayer: Thank you, Father, for the graces of mercy and humility. You, Lord, are merciful and gracious, slow to anger, and plenteous in mercy.[1] I pray for _____ _____, that he/she shall praise you, because your lovingkindness is better than life.[2]

Help him/her to fulfill your joy by being like-minded with you, in fellowship with your Spirit and full of mercy.[3] Let the same mind of humility and obedience be in _____ which was also in Christ Jesus.[4]

Guide him/her to fulfill your will by putting on an attitude of mercy, kindness, humility, humbleness of mind and longsuffering; to forgive as Christ forgave him/her; and above all else, to put on love which is the bond of perfectness.[5]

References: (1) Psalms 103:8; (2) Psalms 63:3; (3) Philippians 2:1-2; (4) Philippians 2:5-8; (5) Colossians 3:12-14.

Walking In Obedience

Key Thought: "Obedience to God is the most infallible evidence of sincere and supreme love to him" (Nathanael Emmons).

Key Scripture: *"Children, obey your parents in the Lord: for this is right. Honour thy father and mother; (which is the first commandment with promise;) That it may be well with thee, and thou mayest live long on the earth" (Eph. 6:1-3).*

Prayer: Heavenly Father, because I want life to go well for my son/daughter and I want him/her to live long upon the earth, I come to you now, asking that you would help me to show him/her the way of obedience to you, first of all, and to me/us, his/her parent(s) as well. May I never be guilty of provoking him/her to wrath, but ever conscious of my responsibility to bring him/her up in your nurture and admonition, Father.[1]

Lead my son/daughter to a saving knowledge of your Son, O Lord.[2] Help him/her to know that his/her love for you will result in obedience to your Word.[3] Show him/her that it is far more important to obey you than it is to obey people.[4] Enable him/her to resist all pressures of the peer group that may go against your will for him/her.

Lord, your Word declares that the willing and obedient ones will be able to eat the good of the land.[5] I claim this promise for my son/daughter as you teach him/her to become obedient. I ask you to grant him/her a wise and obedient heart that will appropriately obey you, authority figures[6] and me/us, his/her parent(s) in all things. As we face these last days, Father, I pray that you will show my son/daughter that when he/she is in tribulation, if he/she will turn to you and be obedient to your voice, you will not forsake him/her and you will not forget your covenant with him/her.[7] Praise your name, O Lord.

To obey you, Father, is better than sacrifices and to hearken to your voice and your teachings is better than riches.[8] Reveal this precious truth to my son/daughter and lead him/her to walk in this truth at all times.

I ask you, Father, O God of peace, who raised our Lord Jesus from the dead, that great Shepherd of the sheep, through the blood of the everlasting covenant, to make my child, _____, complete in every good work to do your will, working in him/her what is well-pleasing in your sight, through Jesus Christ, to whom be glory forever and ever. Amen.[9]

References: (1) Ephesians 6:1-4; (2) John 3:16; (3) John 14:15; (4) Acts 5:29; (5) Isaiah 1:19; (6) Romans 13:1; (7) Deuteronomy 4:30-31; (8) 1 Samuel 15:22; (9) Hebrews 13:21-22, NKJV.

Walking in Patience

Key Thought: The feet that wait for God always arrive at the goal.

Key Scripture: *"That you do not become sluggish, but imitate those who through faith and patience inherit the promises" (Heb. 6:12).*

Prayer: Heavenly Father, so fill the life of my son/daughter, _____, that he/she will always bear the fruit of patience in his/her life.[1] Thank you for providing patience for him/her through the power of your Spirit, and I ask you, Lord, to help me to ever be a model of patience in front of my child. Let him/her know, beyond all doubt, that when he/she does your will, by waiting patiently before you, he she will receive your promise.[2] Teach _____ to learn how to wait on you, Lord.[3] Your way is perfect, and your Word is true.[4] My soul waits for you because you are my help and my shield.[5]

More than they that watch for the morning, I pray that my child's soul will always seek to wait for you, O Lord.[6] Teach him/her to be slow to wrath and to be one who possesses great understanding.[7] Help him/her to always remember that the patient in spirit are better than the proud.[8] Because of your greatness, glory and power, O God, my son/daughter will be able to wait on you, and

I know that you will save him/her because you are the Lord of all.[9]

Thank you for all the precious promises of your Word, O Father. Though it may seem to my son/daughter that your promise may tarry at times, show him/her the importance of waiting for your promise. Give him/her faith and confidence to hold onto the certainty that your promise will surely be fulfilled.[10] Your Word is always true, and your faithfulness is unto all generations.[11]

When tribulation comes to _____, help him/her always to remember that the trials of life produce perseverance; and perseverance, character; and character, hope.[12] Thank you, Lord. Teach my son/daughter never to grow weary in well-doing by revealing to him/her that he/she will reap in due season if he/she will learn to wait for your perfect will to be accomplished.[13]

Teach him/her to be patient toward all other people in his/her life, Lord.[14] Let the fruit of patience in his/her life be evident to all.[15] Guide him/her to be a follower of those who through faith and patience inherit the promises.[16] Lead him/her to let patience have its perfect work in his/her life so that he/she may be perfect and complete, lacking nothing.[17]

References: *(1) Galatians 5:22; (2) Hebrews 10:36; (3) Psalms 130:5; (4) Psalms 18:30; (5) Psalms 33:20; (6) Psalms 130:6; (7) Proverbs 14:29; (8) Ecclesiastes 7:8; (9) Isaiah 25:9; (10) Habakkuk 2:3; (11) Psalms 119:90; (12) Romans 5:3-4, NIV; (13) Galatians 6:9; (14) 1 Thessalonians 5:14; (15) Galatians 5:22; (16) Hebrews 6:12; (17) James 1:4.*

Walking in Peace

Key Thought: Peace of mind comes when one makes his peace with God.

Key Scripture: *"And let the peace of God rule in your hearts, to the which ye are called in one body; and be ye thankful" (Col. 3:15).*

Prayer: God of peace, thank you for your gift of peace which passes all understanding. I pray that your peace will keep the heart of my son/daughter, _____ _____ , through Christ Jesus.[1] Give him/her the peace of mind that comes through you. Keep him/her in perfect peace, Father, by showing _____ _____ that peace comes when one learns to keep his/her mind stayed upon you because he/she trusts you.[2] I pray that _____ will ever keep his/her mind stayed on you and that he/she will trust you always.

Let _____ allow your peace to be the umpire in his/her heart that reveals what is right and wrong to him/her. Help _____ to always follow the guidance your peace gives to him/her in his/her heart.[3]

Help _____ to live in peace with all people.[4] May he/she always remember that there is no excuse for strife and unforgiveness. Help him/her to remember that it takes two to quarrel, and a soft answer always turns wrath away.[5]

Lord, help him/her to keep his/her tongue from evil, to seek peace with all his/her heart,[6] fully realizing that Jesus Christ is the Prince of peace.[7] Lead _____ _____ to always want to follow you with all his/her heart.

Help _____ to be a fruit-bearing Christian, Lord, one who shows forth the fruit of peace in all his/her relationships.[8] As he/she learns to live in your Spirit, help him/her to walk in peace[9] with you, his/her fellow-man, and within himself/herself as well.[10]

Peace is such a precious possession, Lord. Lead _____ to guard it carefully, never permitting anything to disturb the peace you impart to him/her.

Show _____ that when he/she follows your commandments, you will give him/her peace like a river, and your righteousness as the waves of the sea.[11]

References: (1) Philippians 4:7; (2) Isaiah 26:3,4; (3) Colossians 3:15; (4) Romans 12:18; (5) Proverbs 15:1; (6) Psalms 34:13-14; (7) Isaiah 9:6; (8) James 3:18; (9) Galatians 5:25; (10) Hebrews 12:14; (11) Isaiah 48:18.

Walking in Revelation

Key Thought: God loves to give wisdom and revelation to children.

Key Scripture: *"Now we have received, not the spirit of the world, but the Spirit who is from God, that we might know the things that have been freely given to us by God"* *(1 Cor. 2:12, NKJV).*

Prayer: Dear God, the Father of my Lord Jesus Christ and the Father of glory, I thank you for your love and for my child, _____. My prayer is that you would give unto my child the spirit of wisdom and revelation in the knowledge of you, so that the eyes of his/her understanding would be enlightened. May he/she know (and understand) the hope of your calling and what are the riches of the glory of your inheritance in the saints, and may he/she know what is the exceeding greatness of your power toward us who believe, according to the working wrought in Christ when you raised Him from the dead, and set Him at your own right hand in the heavenly places, far above all principality, and power, and might, and dominion, and every name that is named, not only in this world, but also in that which is to come. And you have put all things under His feet and gave Him to be the head over all things to the Church, which is His body, the fullness of Him who fills all in all. Amen.[1]

References: (1) Ephesians 1:17-23.

Walking in Self-Control
(Temperance)

Key Thought: Self-control is possible only when we are controlled by Christ.

Key Scripture: *"He that hath no rule over his own spirit is like a city that is broken down, and without walls" (Prov. 25:28).*

Prayer: Dear Lord, help _____ to know that self-control is an important quality to develop in life and that it is, in fact, a fruit of your Spirit. Fill my son/daughter with your Spirit so that he/she will be able to exercise self-control at all times.[1]

Guide him/her to add to his/her self-control patience, and to his/her patience godliness.[2] I ask you to convince him/her of the need to remain in control by being under your Lordship.

Strengthen _____ by your Spirit, Lord, so that the fruit of self-control will blossom in his/her life.[3] Let him/her strive for the mastery in life by being temperate in all things, to seek the incorruptible crown of life[4] above all else. Help him/her to keep his/her body under subjection to his/her spirit, and to your Spirit, Lord, and as he/she runs the race of life may he/she always look unto Jesus who is the Author and Finisher of our faith.[5]

I pray that _____ will hold fast to the faithful Word that you have given to him/her. Help him/her never to seek self-gratification, but to be just, holy, and temperate.[6] Lead him/her to put on the breastplate of your righteousness, and the helmet of salvation, realizing that these gifts from your hands will help him/her to remain sober and vigilant throughout his/her life.[7] Assist _____ in bringing all his/her thoughts into the captivity of Christ.[8] May He (Christ) so influence his/her life that self-control will actually be the fruit of Christ's Lordship in all things. Thank you for developing and cultivating the fruit of self-control in the life of my son/daughter.

References: *(1) Galatians 5:23; (2) 2 Peter 1:6; (3) Galatians 5:23; (4) 1 Corinthians 9:24-27; (5) Hebrews 12:1,2; (6) Titus 1:7-9; (7) 1 Thessalonians 5:6-8; (8) 2 Corinthians 10:5.*

Walking in Trust

Key Thought: "You may trust the Lord too little, but you can never trust Him too much" (Anonymous).

Key Scripture: *"Trust in the Lord with all thine heart; and lean not unto thine own understanding. In all thy ways acknowledge him, and he shall direct thy paths" (Prov. 3:5-6).*

Prayer: Thank you for the promises of your Word, Father. They are like a concrete sidewalk to walk upon because they are so trustworthy. I pray that my son/daughter, _____ , will learn to trust you with all his/her heart instead of leaning unto his/her own understanding.[1] I ask that his/her heart would be fixed totally in trust of you, for I know that this will keep him/her free from any fear of evil tidings.[2]

May he/she ever retain the childlike quality of trust, growing in your nurture and admonition,[3] being rooted and grounded in your love[4] and constantly increasing in faith without which it is impossible to please you, Father.[5]

Thank you for your promise that states that anyone who trusts in you will become like a tree planted by the waters, that spreads out its roots by the river. It does not fear and it always bears fruit.[6] I pray that _____ _____ will be a tree of your planting, Lord. Lead him/her to drink freely of your waters of life.[7]

As _____ learns to trust in you without reserve, you will direct his/her paths.[8] Your mercy will encompass him/her.[9] Thank you, Father, for your great faithfulness that will lead my son/daughter to trust in you. Watch over him/her throughout his/her life.

Help _____ to know the importance of prayer as a key to trust. Lead him/her to continue in supplications and prayers night and day.[10] Grant that he/she would never trust in uncertain riches or any other thing except you, the living God, who richly gives us all things to enjoy.[11]

As _____ learns to trust you, Lord, I pray that you will help him/her to build other relationships — friendships, business associations, family, marriage, parenting, church — in his/her life that are based on trust. All trust comes from and through you, and as he/she turns to you, help him/her to realize that he/she is not sufficient in anything, but all his/her sufficiency comes from you, and you are making him/her into an able minister of the New Testament,[12] a minister of reconciliation[13] and a person who can be trusted at all times.

References: (1) Proverbs 3:5-6; (2) Psalms 112:7; (3) Ephesians 6:4; (4) Ephesians 3:17; (5) Hebrews 11:6; (6) Jeremiah 17:7-8, NIV; (7) Revelation 21:6; (8) Proverbs 3:6; (9) Psalms 32:10-11; (10) 1 Timothy 5:5; (11) 1 Timothy 6:17-18; (12) 2 Corinthians 3:4-6; (13) 2 Corinthians 5:18.

Walking in Wisdom and Knowledge

Key Thought: Without wisdom, knowledge is of little worth.

Key Scripture: *"My son, eat thou honey, because it is good; and the honeycomb, which is sweet to thy taste; So shall the knowledge of wisdom be unto thy soul"* *(Prov. 24:13-14).*

Prayer: Lord, I thank you for the certainty your Word provides to us, for your Word is forever settled in heaven,[1] and you watch to see that your Word is fulfilled.[2] You have shown us that through wisdom a house is built and by understanding it is established.[3] I pray, dear Father, that my child's home will be built through wisdom and established by understanding, and I ask that he/she will find the strength that wisdom brings.[4]

In your sight, O Lord, a wise child is better than a foolish king,[5] and I ask you to lead my child to your wisdom that gives life to those who have it.[6] Through wisdom, I pray that you will impart strength and vitality to _____.[7]

Let the face of my son/daughter shine with the wisdom you impart to him/her.[8] Fill him/her with wisdom so that his/her heart will be able to discern both time and judgment.[9] Let your light, understanding and excellent wisdom be found in him/her.[10] May he/she ever know that wisdom is better than physical strength,[11] that it has always been better than weapons of war.[12]

I thank you that wisdom and might are yours to give,[13] and I pray that you will grant your wisdom and knowledge to _____.

I ask that the life of my son/daughter will be like the wise man described by Jesus — the man who built his house upon a rock.[14] May he/she always realize that the wisdom of this world is foolishness with you.[15]

As the parent of _____, I ask you for wisdom for myself as well. I thank you, Father, that when we lack wisdom we can come to you, realizing that, if we ask in faith, nothing wavering, you will liberally impart wisdom to us.[16] It is so much better to get wisdom than gold, and I ask you to help me to hold onto this value and to help my son/daughter to give high priority to wisdom as well.[17]

Lord, give wisdom to my son/daughter. Lead him/her to know that knowledge and understanding come forth from your mouth.[18] Teach him/her to number his/her days, that he/she may apply his/her heart unto wisdom.[19] Above all else, Father, I ask that you will show _____ that to fear (respect, revere, honor) you is to experience the beginning of wisdom,[20] and guide him/her to worship you in spirit and in truth.[21]

References: *(1) Psalms 119:89;* *(2) Jeremiah 1:12, NIV; (3) Proverbs 24:3; (4) Eccclesiastes 7:19; (5) Ecclesiastes 4:13; (6) Ecclesiastes 7:12; (7) Ecclesiastes 7:12; (8) Ecclesiastes 8:1; (9) Ecclesiastes*

8:5; (10) Daniel 5:14; (11) Ecclesiastes 9:16; (12) Ecclesiastes 9:18; (13) Daniel 2:20; (14) Matthew 7:24-26; (15) 1 Corinthians 3:19; (16) James 1:5; (17) Proverbs 16:16; (18) Proverbs 2:6; (19) Psalms 90:12; (20) Psalms 111:10; (21) John 4:24.

A Well-Rounded Education

Key Thought: "Prayer moves the hand which moves the world" (John Aikman Wallace).

Key Scripture: *"The fear of the Lord is the beginning of wisdom: a good understanding have all they that do his commandments: his praise endureth forever" (Ps. 111:10).*

Prayer: Heavenly Father, I pray for my child's education, asking you to bring Christian teachers who are full of your wisdom to him/her. Help each of his/her teachers to know and apply the truth of your Word and to realize that the tongue of the wise uses knowledge rightly, but the mouth of fools pours out foolishness.[1]   Bless my child, _____, with a well-rounded education that will enable him/her to grow in positive directions mentally, physically, athletically, emotionally, socially and spiritually.[2]

Continually remind my son/daughter of his/her need to study to show himself/herself approved unto you, a workman who never needs to be ashamed because he/she has learned to rightly divide your Word.[3] Help my child to realize that the individuals who find your wisdom, Lord, and those who gain understanding will always prosper.[4] Help him/her to apply his/her heart to wisdom,[5] and to keep his/her heart with all diligence, for out of the heart are the issues of life. Help my son/daughter to always honor your Word, Father, and to attend to your voice, to incline his/her ears to your sayings, for they are life unto those who find them, and health to all their flesh.[6]

Fill my child with your wisdom, Lord, so that he/she would always be able to discern your will.[7] Help him/her to ever realize that there is strength and wisdom with you, O Lord.[8] In the hidden parts of his/her life, help him/her to know wisdom.[9] Fill him/her with the knowledge of your will in all wisdom and spiritual understanding. This will enable him/her to walk worthy of you, Lord, unto all pleasing and to be fruitful in every good work, always increasing in the knowledge of your ways.[10]

References: *(1) Proverbs 15:2; (2) Matthew 7:7-8; (3) 2 Timothy 2:15; (4) Proverbs 3:13; (5) Psalms 90:12; (6) Proverbs 4:20-23; (7) Exodus 28:3; (8) Job 12:13; (9) Psalms 51:6; (10) Colossians 1:9-11.*

PRAYERS THAT PREVAIL FOR YOUR CHILDREN

Prayer Journal

Prayer Journal

Date	Notes and Comments

Date	Notes and Comments

Date	Notes and Comments

Date	Notes and Comments

Date	Notes and Comments

Date	Notes and Comments

Date	Notes and Comments

Date	Notes and Comments

Prayer Journal

Date	Notes and Comments

Date	Notes and Comments

Date	Notes and Comments

Date	Notes and Comments

Prayer Journal

Date   Notes and Comments

Date	Notes and Comments

Date	Notes and Comments

Date	Notes and Comments

Date	Notes and Comments

Date	Notes and Comments

Date	Notes and Comments

Date	Notes and Comments

Date	Notes and Comments

Date	Notes and Comments

Date	Notes and Comments

Date	Notes and Comments

PRAYER CLASSIC

Pray God's Word - Receive His Promises

Praying God's Word puts His dynamic power to work and energizes your faith. PRAYERS THAT PREVAIL is a practical manual for building an effective prayer life. This essential tool is filled with prayers and scriptures that address more than 100 topics of vital concern to every believer.

ALSO AVAILABLE

☆　　☆　　☆ · 　☆　　☆　　☆

PRAYERS THAT PREVAIL FOR AMERICA–Changing a Nation
Through Prayer: An Intercessor's Manual by the authors of the best-
selling *Prayers That Prevail.* Learn how to pray God's powerful promises
in behalf of our nation, our leaders, our people and our problems. Take
America back through sixty topical prayers from the Bible that invoke
God's blessings and mercy for our land. In addition to the prayers, this
dynamic book includes "A Call to Intercession," a look at "The
Presidents and Prayer," "One Nation Under God," and "Fifty Prayer
Promises." For every Christian who is concerned about America.

ALSO AVAILABLE

You will laugh, feel challenged, learn new truths, and desire to become the best you can be as you take just a few moments to glean fresh insights into God's wisdom and the witty sayings of men and women, past and present.

An ideal giftbook for all occasions, *A Little Bit of God's Wisdom and Wit* will find its way into the hearts, homes and hands of people everywhere.

FOR THE MEN TOO

This handy book has been designed by men for men. Wisdom from the Bible and witty sayings from the pens of men will give the reader insights into life and success.

Small enough to be taken anywhere, a man will enjoy reading this book wherever he may go, providing relief from tension, truths to take hold of, and humor to brighten his day.

Prayer Requests

Your prayer needs are important to us.
If you have a prayer request — just write to
Clift Richards & Lloyd Hildebrand at:

Victory House, Inc.
"Prayers That Prevail"
P.O. Box 700238
Tulsa, OK 74170

BOOK ORDER FORM

To order additional books by Clift Richards and Lloyd Hildebrand direct from the publisher, please use this order form. Also note that your local bookstore can order titles for you.

Book Title	Price	Quantity	Amount
Prayers That Prevail	$ 8.99	_____	$ _____
Prayers That Prevail for America	$ 8.99	_____	$ _____
Prayers That Prevail for Your Children	$ 8.99	_____	$ _____
A Little Bit of God's Wisdom & Wit	$ 5.99	_____	$ _____
A Little Bit of God's Wisdom & Wit for Men	$ 5.99	_____	$ _____

Total Book Amount $ _____

Shipping & Handling — Add $2.00 for the **first** book, **plus** $0.50 for **each** additional book. $ _____

TOTAL ORDER AMOUNT — Enclose check or money order. (No cash or C.O.D.'s.) $ _____

Make check or money order payable to: **VICTORY HOUSE, INC.**
Mail order to: **Victory House, Inc.**
　　　　　　　P.O Box 700238
　　　　　　　Tulsa, OK 74170

Please print your name and address **clearly:**

Name _____

Address _____

City _____

State or Province _____

Zip or Postal Code _____

Telephone Number (___) _____

Foreign orders must be submittted in U.S. dollars. Foreign orders are shipped by uninsured surface mail. We ship all orders within 48 hours of receipt of order.

MasterCard or VISA — For credit card orders you may use your MasterCard or VISA by completing the following information, or for **faster service,** call toll-free **1-800-262-2631**.

Card Name _____

Card Number _____

Expiration Date _____

Signature _____

(authorized signature)